# PORTRA      OF
# PIDDINGHOE

## 1900–2000

*Piddinghoe pictured from the church tower when it was being reshingled in 1980.*

Photo: Village scrapbook

# Valerie Mellor

# S.B. Publications

*For Piddinghoers, past and present*
*and in particular*
*Olive Crooks*
*30 March 1904–28 March 2000*

First published in 2000 by S. B. Publications,
19 Grove Road, Seaford, East Sussex BN25 1TP

ISBN 1 85770 213 1

Designed and typeset by CGB, Lewes
Printed by Tansleys The Printers,
19 Broad Street, Seaford, East Sussex BN25 1LS
Tel: 01323 891019

# Contents

*Front cover:* Local artist Mick Bensley's painting of Piddinghoe c.1950, taken from 'Watercolours of Sussex Past' by Nick Bensley and Bob Copper, published 1998.

*Back cover:* Local artist Edward Bennett's 1923 painting of Piddinghoe by Moonlight. Kindly loaned by Derek Smith.

# ACKNOWLEDGEMENTS

This book could not have been written without the assistance of many Piddinghoers, past and present. I am particularly grateful for the unstinting support of Pat Smith and her many hours of work copying, and transcribing on to disk, documents from the Public Record Office and East Sussex Record Office. To the late Olive Crooks I am indebted for hours of entertaining taped conversations, which inspired me to find out more about the village and parish which meant so much to her. To all the many others who have given so willingly of their memories and time, it is a pleasure to record my sincere thanks.

I am also deeply grateful to Sid Alce, the late Olive Crooks, the Harrison family, Terry Hollands, Jo Jenner, Sheila Lower, Bert Luke, Alistair Moon, Mary Murray, Newhaven Historical Society, Peggy Pawson, the late Molly Pelling, Winnie Smart, Pat Smith, Richard Way and Mary Woolger for the loan of photographs. My thanks, too, to Susan Rowland who drew the maps and Edward Reeves of Lewes who copied so many of the original photographs. A number of the pictures in this book are from the village scrapbooks as indicated in the captions.

Despite all this assistance, any errors, omissions or shortcomings belong exclusively to the author.

# ABOUT THE AUTHOR

Valerie Mellor has lived in Piddinghoe since 1985, after many years in Brighton and a childhood in Birmingham.

Since her retirement from the Faculty of Education Studies at Brighton Polytechnic in 1990, she has taken an active role in village life. Formerly a professional geographer, she has now become an amateur local historian and is engrossed in Piddinghoe.

# INTRODUCTION

The incentive for this book came from the belief that, while actual and inherited memories remained, a record should be made of Piddinghoe in the twentieth century. The aims are twofold. First, to enable Piddinghoers, present and past, to know more about their parish. Second, to offer the general reader some insight into the last hundred years of life in this Sussex village, the detail of which illustrates many of the general themes underlying rural areas at this time.

In 1900 the parish constituted a community, forced by its comparative isolation to be largely self sufficient. In 2000, despite easy access to distant places, it is a community still and one in which, on an occasion such as Millennium Day on 24 June this year, almost every villager physically capable of joining in the festivities, chose so to do.

Inevitably, the community and its environment today are substantially different from what they were in 1900. The transition from one to the other forms the substance of this book. Each decade demonstrates both continuity and change – an evolving portrait of Piddinghoe.

**Valerie Mellor**
**Old Post Office**
**Piddinghoe**
**July 2000**

'Time present and time past
Are both perhaps present in time future,
And time future contained in time past.'
    T S Eliot. *Four Quartets* 'Burnt Norton

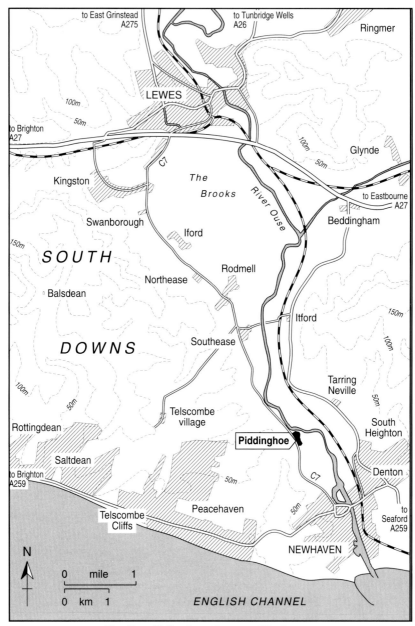

**The Ouse Valley from Lewes to Newhaven.**

# 1

# SETTING THE SCENE

PIDDINGHOE – Saxon name meaning spur of land (either hill or jutting into water) belonging to Pydda's people. Traditionally pronounced Pidd'noo, remembered by the rhyme:
*Englishmen fight, Frenchmen too;*
*We doant, we live in Pidd'noo!'*

The parish of Piddinghoe, in 1900, included all the land now occupied by Peacehaven, its southern boundary comprising a two-mile stretch of wild and lonely coastline from which sheer chalk cliffs plunged 100 feet or more to the sea below. At night coastguards patrolled the cliff top on the look out for smugglers. Daylight would reveal hummocky grass and gorse on the seaward side of the narrow rough-surfaced Dover Road, now the A259. Inland, rolling chalk downland stretched as far as the eye could see. Signs of life were few. Just two isolated cottages and, in the distance, the group of buildings that formed Hoddern Farm. In contrast

**Piddinghoe from Harping Hill. Court House farm is on the right.**

7

**The Brick and Whiting Works pictured in its heyday in the 1880s.**
*Photo: Reeves of Lewes*

the northern edge of the parish, fringing the Ouse Valley, hummed with activity. Here was the village with its Brick and Whiting Works, Deans and Court House farms, the main Lewes to Newhaven road and the river itself.

The parish started – and ended – the century with a population of 231, much the same as in the previous eighty years. The majority lived in the village, with its thirty four houses, church, school, post office, stores, forge and pub. The houses ranged in size from small eighteenth and nineteenth terraced cottages, to a few, somewhat larger, individual houses dating from the fifteenth and sixteenth centuries. The oldest cottage, part of the old vicarage on the Green, was built in the thirteenth century. St John's church, one of three with a round tower in the Ouse valley, had undergone major restoration work eighteen years previously and light filtering through its modern stained-glass windows lit an immaculate interior. The parishes of Piddinghoe and Telscombe formed a united benefice, the vicar of Piddinghoe being also the rector of Telscombe. Next to the church was the National School built in 1879. At the turn of the century, it housed some forty-six children.

Most river traffic passed, rather than docked, at Piddinghoe. A few

8

sea-going ships made their way up to Lewes and so did a number of spritsail barges, usually with cargoes of timber or coal. The main road to the coast threaded its way through the village. It was a busy road, and getting busier as a result of the improvements to Newhaven harbour.

The three main farms of the parish lay parallel to each other. Deans and Hoddern farms were part of the Earl of Chichester's estate and had fine old farmhouses, each almost certainly older than the sixteenth and seventeenth dates accorded to them. They also had twelve cottages between them, with estate numbers of 109 to 120. Court House to the east, which was owned by the Earl of Sheffield,

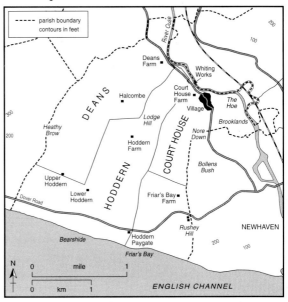

also had a substantial farmhouse dating from at least the seventeenth century but with later additions. Its great barn and two cottages, Townsend and Pear Tree, lined the Street. By 1900, unlike the Chichester farms, some of the Court House land was sublet, ten per cent to Malthouse farm in the village and about thirty per cent – Friar's Bay Farm at the seaward end – to the nearby New Barn farm in Newhaven.

The parish at this time had no mains services. Water had to be drawn from one of the wells; sanitation was an outside privy, often shared with nearby cottages; and oil lamps and candles were relied on for providing light at night. There was no public transport so to get anywhere most people had to walk . . .

At the turn of the century this was a self-contained village encompassed by and in harmony with its Sussex downland setting.

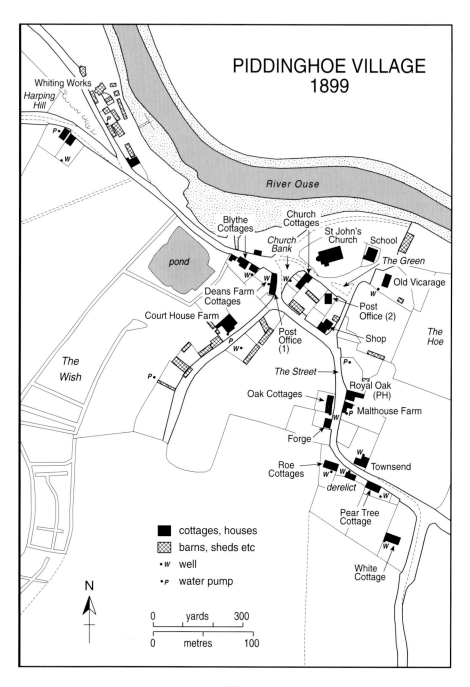

# PIDDINGHOE VILLAGE
## 1899

Whiting Works

*Harping Hill*

P

P•

•w

*River Ouse*

Blythe Cottages

Church Cottages

St John's Church

School

*Church Bank*

*pond*

*The Green*

•w •w •w •w

Deans Farm Cottages

Old Vicarage

•w

Court House Farm

Post Office (2)

Post Office (1)

*The Hoe*

P•

•w

Shop

P•

*The Wish*

P•

*The Street* →

Oak Cottages

Royal Oak (PH)

•P

Malthouse Farm

•w

Forge

•w

Roe Cottages

Townsend

•w

•w •w

*derelict*

•w

Pear Tree Cottage

| | cottages, houses |
| --- | --- |
| | barns, sheds etc |
| •w | well |
| •P | water pump |

White Cottage

•w

N

| 0 | yards | 300 |
| --- | --- | --- |
| 0 | metres | 100 |

10

# 2

# INTO A NEW CENTURY

## 1900–1909

Officially Britain entered the twentieth century on 1 January 1901, three weeks before the death of Queen Victoria in the sixty-fourth year of her reign. The near coincidence of the two events intensified the public view that they heralded the end of an era. Victoria had ruled over the most extensive Empire ever known, and her citizens were perceived as providing leaders in all the major fields of human endeavour. Some commentators, however, could see difficulties ahead for the new king, Edward VII, and his people. The Boer War dragged on in South Africa and the German Navy was beginning to threaten Britain's traditional supremacy at sea. At home the increasing militancy of the trade unions and the emergence of Keir Hardie's Independent Labour Party was felt by many employers to be unsettling the workers.

Notwithstanding these concerns, a new age of technology was dawning. The motor car was becoming accepted – not since 1896 had it had to be preceded by a man with a red flag. Speed was the great novelty. In 1901 Marconi bridged the Atlantic by wireless telegraph and eight years later Louis Bleriot piloted his tiny plane across the English Channel. Newspapers were forecasting a great future for electricity.

Life for most of the people in the parish of Piddinghoe did not get any easier during the first decade of the new century. In one respect at least, it became harder, as more people were crammed into the same homes and more children into the same school. A number of the children born in the 1880s and 1890s had stayed in the village and raised their own

11

Back row, l to r: Ernest, Elizabeth 'Bessie', Edgar, Nell (Burdett), Grace (Paddy) and
Jack. Middle row: Sidney 'Rookie', Steve, May (Stevens), Elsie, Olive (Stace), Alice
'Sis' (Boyle), Harold and Tom. Sitting on the grass in front of their father
and mother are Kathleen 'Topsy' (Chivers), Dick and Percy.
*Photo: Village scrapbook*

families. Pre-eminent were the Penfolds and the Alces. James and
Elizabeth Penfold kept the post office, initially opposite Church Bank,
later on the Green. They are pictured above, probably in 1899 on the
occasion of their thirtieth wedding anniversary, with the seventeen
children they had between 1869 and 1893. Only Jack Penfold moved
far away – to Australia. The descendants of eight of the others are still in
the vicinity, at Piddinghoe, Newhaven and Lewes.

The year 1893 also saw the appearance of the first of the seventeen

12

Alces, but they were divided between two step-brothers – Dan and Mary's eight being born between 1893 and 1903, Jim and Edith's nine between 1894 and 1915. As all these Alces became part of the village community they were joined by twenty two second generation Penfolds.

Conditions for couples with large families living in small cottages were primitive. After their marriage in 1896 Ernest and Rhoda Penfold lived in one of the one-up-one-down terraced cottages on Harping Hill and brought up seven children, sleeping everyone in two double beds and a mattress on top of two yellow blanket boxes (part of every woman's trousseau) which sat on the tiny landing. Last thing at night the men of the parish would draw next day's water from the nearest well, often two cottages distant. Every second or third day they had to empty the privy bucket into the river or over the wall into a field. Visiting the privy at night was clearly remembered by the late Mrs Olive Crooks, then Olive Paddy of 3 Blythe cottages.

'Scary it was. Should you light your candle indoors and risk it blowing out ?
Or feel your way across the backs of the other houses, at least then being sure
of a light once there ?'

Work opportunities for men and women changed little over the decade. Farming was just beginning to emerge from a period of depression, but there were still more men than jobs and wages were lower than in the towns. The Piddinghoe farms were, essentially, mixed farms. Crops occupied the lower slopes, with the better soils, and generally were grown on the four-year Norfolk rotation of cereals interspersed with a fodder crop. Large flocks of sheep grazed the downland, their shepherds living an isolated life for most of the year, although animals needing fattening had to be brought down to be 'folded' on fields of crops such as rape or kale. The heavy clays of the Brooklands produced valuable crops of hay, although cattle were turned out on them for part of the year. Most of the men worked on the land – a few specialists as carters, shepherds and cowmen, but most as labourers who could turn their hands to almost any farm job. A few men were employed at the Brick and Whiting Works and by the Lower Ouse Navigation Board. Others walked to the docks, railway and ships at Newhaven or beyond to the

**The Royal Oak in 1904. Standing outside with the mother's help is Ted Bennett and his wife Martha with three of their children.**

thriving cement works at South Heighton. Children were considered part of the work force – stone-picking, watching animals or helping with the harvest. Six year old Olive Paddy earned a halfpenny at the Whiting Works on Saturday mornings for the horse pulling the sledge that crushed the lumps of chalk would only keep going if he was led round and round, even by a child.

A new development was in Plough Brooks, a field beyond the Hoe. One day in 1903 two or three men appeared and began to dig trenches across the bottom of the field next to the river. They were employed by the Lewes Portland Cement Company and the clay they were digging was destined for the Southerham Cement Works. Before long they were joined by Ted Bennett, licensee of the Royal Oak, who had previously been a fireman on the old Newhaven to Caen steamers. Digging the heavy, sticky clay with hand spades was hard and dirty work and the tough moleskin trousers they wore were their only protection against the water which continually seeped into the trenches. From Plough Brooks the clay was taken up stream by barges propelled by two men with quants poling the heavy vessel along, helped by the power of the flood tide.

Work occupied six and a half days of the week, and for some, such as the carters, seven. The men spent the light evenings in their gardens, raising as much produce as possible, with, perhaps, some for sale. Three villagers worked small market gardens and sold any surplus in Newhaven or Seaford – vegetables and fruit in summer, home-killed pork, sausages, chicken and rabbits in winter. Only after all their work was done could they escape to the Royal Oak for a pint or two of Towner's ale, leaving the women at home minding the children, fingers still busy with mending, sewing or knitting and eyes straining in the lamplight.

Visible from the Royal Oak was the shop, run by Frank and Mary Latter from about 1900, when it had already been in Mrs Latter's family for some forty years. Mary Brockway, the Latter's daughter, remembers what it was like:

'It had a thatched roof and a lovely front garden, and was a great attraction for artists. A variety of goods were sold, mostly in halfpenny and pennyworths. Nearly everything was sold loose, such as tea, sugar, rice, peas and all kinds of spices. On Monday mornings mothers sent for their halfpenny worths of soda, starch, borax, and 1lb of soap for  tuppence halfpenny to do the weekly wash. Many items in the way of sweets were sold for a farthing.'

On Sundays attendance at church and Sunday School was expected. Indeed the Church – from 1901 in the person of the Reverend Frederic

15

Poole – was a potent force in parish life. In addition to taking weekly and extra seasonal services, coping with a choir of some fourteen men and six boys and a thriving Sunday School, the vicar was closely involved in all the organised social activity of the parish. In 1903 he was chairman of the thirty-strong management committee responsible for organising the village fair and bazaar. It was opened by the Countess of Chichester and there was a maypole dance, baby show, jumble sale, washing competition, a men's hat trimming competition, bicycle races and a threading the needle race. The adult entrance fee for each contest was threepence, except for the race for the greasy pig scheduled to take place at 7.45pm – that was one shilling. Music of a military flavour, interspersed with the occasional waltz, gavotte, polka and schottische, was provided by Seaford Town Band. In the same year this energetic vicar started the village club and in January 1904 the *Telscombe and Piddinghoe Parish Magazine.* In the first issue he covered a range of topics, reporting on 'club matches of whist, cribbage, bagatelle and draughts with Rodmell and the Newhaven Harbour Fire Brigade' and announcing that 'the village library in connection with this club is now open'.

Perhaps Mr Poole's most ambitious project in Piddinghoe was the building of the reading room. It was not all plain sailing. In the August 1905 issue of the parish magazine he declared that:

'I hope that in the course of a few weeks there will be a Parish room at Piddinghoe, available for the Village Club when it reopens on October 2nd, for the library, and for other Parochial purposes.'

However in October –

'I hoped that the Parish room at Piddinghoe would have been completed by now, but I see no prospect of the contractor being able to finish his work at the date agreed upon.'

But in November –

'I am glad to say that the Parish Room at Piddinghoe is in use and paid for. I hope to make arrangements early in the month for a Mothers' Meeting and working party to be held weekly during the winter months . . . The kindness of those friends who have contributed to the new room enable me to transfer the amounts received from the Concert and from the Primrose League fete to the organ repairing fund, and thus with the aid of the jumble sale, to get out of debt at once.'

This small room with its polished match-boarding interior was built in the front garden of the Old Vicarage, to the left of the path. It was to serve as the parochial and village hall for the next fifty years. The library flourished. After only one year it had 500 books and in the twelve months prior to July 1906 a total of 2,220 loans had been made and only one volume was missing. By the end of the decade the number of books had risen to 750. The village club, too, went from strength to strength. Annual home and away matches of whist, cribbage and bagatelle continued against Rodmell, Iford, South Heighton Cement Works, Newhaven Harbour Fire Brigade, and occasionally Southease and Denton. In 1909 Piddinghoe won the newly-formed Whist and Cribbage League, beating South Heighton into second place.

In the summer cricket took over. A full programme of home and away

**Children and adults turned out in force every year to watch the camels and elephants of Sanger's Circus as they were led by their trainers through the village on their way to Newhaven. It was there, in 1904, that Jim Alce's milk horse took fright at the scent of the camels and bolted. The animal was so badly injured it had to be destroyed. A successor is pictured above outside Malthouse Farm.**

matches was played each year against a variety of local sides. Although the team did not win any trophies there were exciting matches, none more so than in 1906 and 1907 when three consecutive contests between Piddinghoe and Rodmell provided nail-biting finishes. As much enjoyed as the games was the annual club supper held each autumn at the Royal Oak.

The lives of children during this decade in many ways mirrored those of the adults. The church affected their lives, perhaps, even more strongly than those of their parents, and they had much less time for play than today's children. The school, built to accommodate fifty two, had sixty nine pupils by 1906. They ranged in age and size from tiny infants to strapping fourteen year olds and were packed into one room measuring 36ft by 18ft by 20ft. For most of the decade there were two classes, separated by a thin, removable partition. 'The infants were down the river end, the oldest nearest the Green. It was really crowded and were we pleased to go out outside at playtime', said Olive Crooks, née Paddy, who was a pupil there from 1909.

From the children's point of view, one of the best days of the school year was 19 July, the date of Little Edith's Treat. It was one of the three Croft Bequests set up by Mrs Elizabeth Croft after the deaths, between 1866 and 1869 of her husband, her grandchild aged three months, and her only son. She left £350 consolidated stock in trust for the 'benefit of the poor of the parish' – the date of each bequest to commemorate the birthday of the person concerned.

The Hugh Croft's Gifts were presented on 19 January each year to the heads of families and widows who were regular churchgoers and 'keep their houses in an orderly and clean condition'. On 22 February the Gilmore Croft's Rewards were given to three single men and to three single women aged 17–30 years, the sons and daughters of parishioners, who could produce 'the most satisfactory character from their employers'. Finally, on 19 July, came the Little Edith Treat 'for the children of the National School' together with 'rewards, more especially to girls skilled in plain needlework, and to the boys and girls who are neat, clean and regular attenders at Church and School'.

In the 1904 parish magazine it was reported that:

> 'There was a good substantial tea for the children, about 70 in all, to which ample justice was done. In addition to this there was a plentiful supply of biscuits, sweets, and nuts, and Prizes were awarded for regular attendance, needlework and drawing.'

The fund for the Little Edith Treat is still in existence – and the event itself has proved to be of interest to the world outside the village as Olive Crooks' son Ken, discovered in April 1997. He was listening to the *Pam Ayres Show* on Radio 2 and heard someone in Harlow appealing for information about the treat. He saw to it that all the details were sent to the BBC and the story of Piddinghoe's Croft Bequests was broadcast on a subsequent *Pam Ayres Show*.

The village school, attended by children from across the parish, was managed by the church, albeit after 1902 in conjunction with the local education authority. It was built by the National Society for the Education of the Poor in the Principles of the Established Church, hence the name 'National School'. Religious knowledge formed a significant part of the curriculum and its teaching was assessed annually by a diocesan inspection. In the church today is a reminder of the children of Piddinghoe at this time, in the shape of the font cover. The inscription round the edge reads: 'This cover was presented by the children of the parish 1904 and 1905'. The total cost was £5 13s 4d (£5.65p).

Each year a Flower Service was held. The children gathered flowers from their gardens and surrounding fields and woods and at evensong on Trinity Sunday they would stand in the aisle singing the hymn *Here Lord we offer Thee all that is fairest*, before going up with their offerings. The following morning the headmistress, Mrs Lucy Baker, would send the flowers to Plaistow Fever Hospital in East London and back would come a letter from the matron thanking Piddinghoe for 'sending real country flowers . . . they are giving great pleasure to our little East End children.'

The children would be on flower duty at some village weddings as well. When Minnie Carr, the daughter of Harry Carr of Court House Farm and Edward Holman of Tarring Neville left St John's church after their wedding on 22 April 1908 their way was strewn with flowers by

**There were flowers, family pets and everyone in their finery for the uniting of two farming families at the wedding of Edward Holman and Minnie Carr.**
*Photo: Edward Reeves, Lewes.*

**Queuing for a ride on the roundabout set up in a field at Telscombe for the Sunday School treat on 3 August 1907.**

girls of the Sunday School who lined each side of the path. The bride had taught at the school since it reopened in 1901 and on Easter Day her fellow teachers and the children gave her a handsome lamp. The parish magazine reported that Bessie Aukett, who had not missed an attendance at the school since the reopening, made 'a happy little speech' as she made the presentation.

It was assumed that, if they had reasonable singing voices, the boys would join the choir and, when strong enough, pump the organ. All children were expected to go to Sunday School where there was yet another treat in store for them. It was held at Telscombe, where philanthropist Ambrose Gorham had his racing stables. He provided amusements for the children – and for their elders too – in the shape of a roundabout, swings and coconut shies, to say nothing of races and presents of sweets and apples. The adults had their tea after the children had finished, and they in turn were followed by the cricketers who had been playing a match in the afternoon.

The large numbers of children in the village meant that none of them lacked companions of their own age or something to do. The countryside provided opportunities for exploration and play but it was a countryside which, before too long, would be transformed.

21

# 3

# TROUBLED TIMES

## 1910–1919

Nine years after the death of Queen Victoria, the nation was mourning the loss of Edward VII. In his short reign he had established himself as a reassuringly steadfast figurehead, in times which were more disturbed than the popular view of Edwardian England might suggest. George V inherited a country, in some respects, at war with itself. Mrs Pankhurst's suffragettes were at the height of their campaign of disobedience and destruction in their pursuit of votes for women. The army was used to keep the peace in three unrelated incidents in 1910 and 1911, in one of which two striking Liverpool dockers were killed. Even this, however, shrank into insignificance on 4 August 1914 when England declared war on Germany. What became known as the 'Great War' had begun and men rushed to join up. By September half a million had done so, with no idea of what horrors were in store for them. At home, some of the gaps they left in the work force were, whenever possible, filled by women.

Piddinghoe did not escape the effects of the war, neither those who went to fight nor those who stayed at home. Locally there were other significant developments, some completed in this decade, others begun, their impact to be felt in later years. It was not, however, all change. For the vast majority life at home and at work continued to be a struggle. The prosperity and gaiety commonly associated with the Edwardian era had largely passed them by and the accession of a new monarch signalled no break with the past.

As in the previous ten years, some seventy five per cent of the men worked on the land, most of them as labourers. Cattle were becoming more important than previously, since, until 1914, the price of imported wheat undercut the home market. Dairy cows had been introduced to the Ouse Valley back in 1895 by a farmer at Iford and, now others were following his lead. Albert Evenden, his wife and four youngest children, came from Barcombe to set up a small dairy unit, renting Townsend Cottage and land from Court House Farm. Some men had regular employment, others were casuals repeatedly having to look for work. The Whiting Works closed down in about 1913 but at the other end of the village the area of clay-working in Plough Brooks grew. Men still dug the clay by hand and had to pole the heavy barges upstream on the flood, returning empty on the ebb tide.

A few women and girls also worked on the land, but the majority entered domestic service. Wealthy people were kept in comfort by an army of domestic servants. There was a complicated and rigid hierarchy 'below stairs'. Female domestics answered to the housekeeper, given the courtesy title of 'Mrs', from lady's maid, to housemaids, to kitchen maids, and the scullion who washed the dishes. Unless they found an opening through a relative or friend the girls would sign on at Saxby House, the Register Office in Seaford.

Olive Paddy left school at the age of thirteen and began the weekly routine of walking to Newhaven then taking the train, fare fourpence to Seaford to see what jobs were available. In February 1918 she started work as a 'tweeny' with a professional family at Lewes for a wage of £16 a year. The house had two huge kitchens in the basement, each used every other week. Nearly everything in them was either steel, which had to be rubbed with emery paper until it shone, or iron which required black-leading. Other jobs included scrubbing the white-wood back stairs from attic to basement, and all the long, dark passages. Olive had one half day off a week, the first of which she spent with an aunt and uncle in Lewes. After a fortnight she was given the Sunday afternoon and evening off and came home as fast as she could, vowing never to return. In spite of her tears her mother insisted that she had to go back and work

23

out her month's notice. The eldest of Ted Bennett's family, Queenie, became a kitchen maid at the same age and the treatment she received from the cook caused her to warn her younger sisters never to follow in her footsteps.

Tradespeople visited the village, mostly from Newhaven, Lewes or Brighton. Twice daily, except Sunday, the mailman called at the post office in his horse-drawn van, bringing letters for delivery to the whole parish in the morning, collecting the sealed postbag in the evening. The carrier came through daily on his way between Lewes and Newhaven, less often the butcher from Rodmell and the fish man with his barrow from Newhaven. When sent for, the doctor came from Newhaven in his pony and trap. There was also an old tinker who sharpened knives, a man who repaired rush seats, and a hurdy-gurdy man, complete with monkey. Thus some aspects of life continued much as before, but others changed irrevocably.

One of the most significant changes of the century was the arrival of mains water. In March 1911 Newhaven Rural District Council ordered the closure of four village wells, on the assumption that the Newhaven and Seaford Water Company would extend their pipe from Newhaven to Piddinghoe. The parish council was outraged, voting four to one against the imposition of this financial burden on the ratepayers. There was uproar at the annual parish meeting on 21 March and it was faithfully reported by the *East Sussex News*. When Dr Hugh Stott, Newhaven's Medical Officer of Health, said that Piddinghoe's water was polluted, all the wells were tidal and river water was not suitable for drinking one villager shouted: 'You ought to be ashamed to say so' and there was a loud 'Hear, hear' from former village school headmistress, Mrs Lucy Baker.

'There have been cases of typhoid fever, as well as many sufferers from sore throats,' continued Dr Stott.

This brought Mrs Baker to her feet again:.

'I deny there have been sore throats and others can say so too.'

'I form my opinion on facts, and I don't expect you to controvert me when you know nothing at all about these things,' said the Medical Officer of Health.

'I do know about sore throats. We have had the best attendance at Piddinghoe School in the district. We who live here ought to know something about it,' said Mrs Baker.

Three days later an independent analyst examined the well water and reported that he could not recommend any of it for drinking. The wells in question were closed and the five guinea bill for the water analysis sent to the parish council. The main from Newhaven was extended to the Whiting Works by a 4inch. diameter pipe under the road and the following year a 3inch pipe took the supply to the house and three cottages on Harping Hill. Village children were fascinated when the workmen came to dig the trench along The Street. In no time they were using a hoop stick to prise up the lid of a manhole cover, one getting her fingers trapped in the process. The delight of having a tap inside the house, however, made up for anything. It was just a tap, no sink and no drain, but little short of a miracle just the same.

In school too, the children's lives were made more comfortable, by the opening, in September 1911, of the long-awaited infant classroom, built to accommodate thirty children at a cost of £460. Ironically, the number of pupils which had given rise to the threat of closure of the school, was never again reached. The fifty five on the roll in April 1915 was the highest of the decade, and then numbers fell until the school closed. With Miss Parker and the infants now in their new room, Miss King and the juniors shared the main room with the head mistress and the seniors, a movable partition between

This picture of the school staff was taken in 1910 by Mary Poole, the vicar's daughter. L to r: Headmistress and seniors, Miss Ella Pearman; juniors, Miss Lilian King; and infants, Miss Martha Parker.

25

them. For the seniors it could have been an unsettling time since, between 1911 and 1915 there were five headteachers, two of whom found the school difficult and stayed for less than a year. In 1915, however, Miss Daisy Iris Porter arrived and stayed for eight years.

Being a church school, religious festivals were strictly kept, including Ash Wednesday and Ascension Day, when, after a service in church, school was dismissed for the day. Good Friday, too, began with a church service followed by dismissal for the Easter holidays. The day was then largely devoted to long-rope skipping. Quite why people skip on Good Friday has never been satisfactorily explained. It appears to be a maritime custom perhaps associated with the drying out of ropes and nets. In Piddinghoe the children, unconcerned about the origin of the exercise, started skipping on the Green in the morning, the strongest ones turning the heavy waggon rope. In the evening, outside the Royal Oak, everyone joined in, five or six at a time, some expertly running in and out of the turning rope.

**A favourite place to play was the Muddy Islands on the left of the path. Blythe Cottages are on the right and Gertie and Katie Penfold are the children posing patiently for the photographer.**

26

**York Cottage and the Compasses, the first two cottages built in Friar's Bay, with their own wind-powered water pump.**

May 1 was Garland Day and the children carried flower-decorated crosses and hoops from house to house, chanting:'The first of May is Garland Day, Please would you like to see our garlands?' Later in May came Empire Day and the whole school assembled on the Green and the 'best boy' had the honour of raising the Union Jack up a makeshift flagpole. After school and in the holidays, strunking was a favourite pastime. The youngsters would go up onto the hills, preferably when the gorse had been burned, and collect the blackened remains which were the sought-after strunks, excellent for lighting the fire under the copper.

The children were blissfully unaware that the hills over which they roamed were under threat. In 1912 the Chichester land came onto the market. Hoddern Farm was bought by the Cavendish Land Company, which promptly sold the whole of the coastal end to Charles Neville for what, in February 1917, was to become Peacehaven. Friar's Bay Farm, previously part of Court House farm, had been put up for sale in 1910.

A substantial plot was bought by Arthur Harrison, founder of the Friar's Bay Smallholders' Co-operative Colony. He built his first two cottages on the site in 1911 – they are still standing – and others soon followed. Arthur himself settled into Shirley Cottage and from there, on 9 January 1917, he wrote to the bailiff at Hoddern Farm:

> 'I presume your shepherd boy will have told you about the damage your sheep have done to my Brussel sprouts, cabbages and winter greens. I estimate the damage done at 25s. . . you will also see the footprints of your sheep all over the garden. . .'

There is no record of a reply.

A fortnight before the outbreak of war land agents Payne, Hurst and Company laid on a special sale train, with luncheon provided, to bring prospective purchasers from London to an auction in a marquee on the Friar's Bay Estate of fifty freehold building plots. So began the later much-derided development of this two-mile stretch of the Channel coast which remained part of Piddinghoe parish until 1929.

Deans and the northern part of Hoddern remained as farms. Harry Carr, whose family had farmed Sussex soil for more than 300 years, bought Deans in 1912 having been tenant farmer at Court House, pictured below, for fourteen years. William Joslin stayed at Hoddern

until 1915 when it came into the ownership of Captain Molyneux Clarke of the Newhaven Garrison. On 25 September of that year offered at auction were:

'Pure-bred and hardy registered hill flock of 974 Southdown sheep; all the flock appliances; capital implements and machinery, including a 6hp petrol engine. About 100 head of poultry and three valuable farm horses, Don, Turpin and Darkie.'

The Great War affected Piddinghoe as it did the whole country but with the added urgency that sometimes the boom of the big guns in France could be heard from the cliff top. Newhaven became the main supply port for the Western Front and to enter its Special Military Area it was necessary to have a permit book like the one, pictured right, which was issued to Alice Thompsett, the twenty two year old daughter of Luke Thompsett of Court House Farm, who with her pony, Peggy, between the shafts drove a milk cart daily to the port.

Many men were in reserved occupations, either working on the land or at Newhaven harbour, but even so some twenty five left the village for active service, among them the vicar, the Reverend George Street, who became an army chaplain. One family had three of its sons in France, six had two and one both father and son. At least seven who went away to war were aged eighteen or younger.

29

Two of them did not return. In May 1918 Mr and Mrs D Alce of 3 Roe Cottages, parents of 22 year old Gunner Frederick Alce of the Royal Field Artillery, received this letter, signed by 2nd Lieutenant H G Beard:

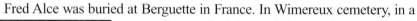

'It is with the greatest regret that I have to inform you that your son, Gunner F.C. Alce has died of wounds received in action on May 1st. He was the signaller of the battalion and a particularly good one at that . . . Four shells fell about 20 yards from us. Your son was hit in the head, stomach and hand . . . The doctor told me he had no chance and I received a note this morning that he died at the Casualty Clearing Station. He was an awfully plucky boy and never complained once. Please accept the sympathy of all the officers, N.C.Os and men of the battery in your great loss.

Fred Alce was buried at Berguette in France. In Wimereux cemetery, in a

grave also marked by a plain wooden cross, lies Stanley Evenden, second son but tenth child of Albert and Harriet Evenden of Townsend Farm. He was only nineteen when he died in France in February 1918.

Although regular farm workers did not go into the armed forces casual labourers did. As a result more girls worked on the land, and German prisoners-of-war were brought each day by guards from Lewes prison. At Malthouse farm they and the family got along quite well together, young Dick Alce learning to count to ten in German.

Horses were requisitioned, which was a great blow as they were vital to farm work. At Malthouse they were able to take back two which had been wounded. A great puzzle to Dick was that the horses could understand the German commands just as well as the English. In 1915 County War Agricultural Committees were set up and some of the Deans and Hoddern land, having become derelict, were among the largest acreages in East Sussex to be farmed by a 'War Ag' committee.

**The army often brought men and its horses up from Newhaven to the slipway by the
school for training exercises.**

Also in 1915 came a development which had more visual impact on the
northern end of the parish than anything else this century, and which
would later significantly change village life. In that year work started on
the construction of the new road to bypass Piddinghoe. Improvements to
the Lewes-Newhaven road were being discussed as early as 1909, when
the National Road Board identified it as an one of its essential projects,
for which it would provide fifty per cent of the funding. In 1910 this was
agreed as £16,000. East Sussex County Council and Newhaven Rural
District Council were to provide £8,000 each, the bypass being part of
the overall scheme.

Work had to be abandoned in 1916, since neither men nor materials
were available. Until almost the end of the decade a great eyesore in the
landscape existed, going nowhere, with wooden barriers at each end.
Although it bypassed the village, it sliced right through the heart of

31

Court House Farm, passing within feet of the house itself, and separating it from its stackyard and cowsheds. Where previously the land had sloped gently to the river, now a solid viaduct was built across the Wish, the valley alongside Court House. Every passing vehicle was now almost level with the upstairs windows of this fine house.

When the war ended it was expected that the workmen would return, which they did, but not until 1919. Horses, too, were demobilised. Fred Durrant, who was then at Townsend, paid £40 to buy back Old Tom from the army. When he went to collect the animal from Lewes he found that it was not at all well. After the walk home it did not look as if Old Tom would last much longer so in desperation, Fred poured a whole bottle of rum down the horse's throat. It did the trick, and Old Tom spent the rest of his days with the WD stamp of his military service still visible on his hindquarters.

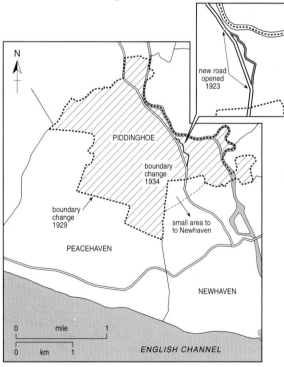

Map showing the boundary changes of 1929, when Peacehaven became a separate parish, and 1934 when a small area to the south-east of Piddinghoe was transferred to Newhaven.
It also shows the line of the Lewes to Newhaven main road through the village and the bypass which was completed in 1923.

# 4

# POST WAR PROBLEMS

## 1920–29

The Great War cast its shadow over much of this third decade of the century. Lists of the fallen appeared in column after closely-printed column in the newspapers. Every year at 11am on 11 November the country fell silent for two minutes. The brief post-war economic boom was fading fast even before all the men were demobilised, so many went straight from the army to the dole queue. The Christmas of 1920 was particularly bleak. World-wide recession cut both jobs and wages resulting in strikes at the docks, on the railways, in the shipyards and the coalmines, and eventually, in 1926, the short-lived General Strike.

But this was also the decade of the frivolous, of the flapper, that slim, shingle-haired antithesis of the Edwardian beauty, and the Charleston, in its early days banned from respectable dance halls. It also marked the beginning of the consumer age, with telephones, telegrams and talking pictures, Austin Sevens, Morris Minors and wireless sets.

Life in the village and on the farms continued much as it had for years, except for the effects of Peacehaven and the new road. Work had re-started on the road in 1919 and stopped again in May 1920 when the workforce came out on strike. It resumed after three months with the employment of ex-service men who were housed in huts at Southease. Lewes Borough Council complained that its end of the road was being ruined by the heavy lorries carrying material to Piddinghoe, only to be told by the county council that no damage would have been caused had its section been given adequate foundations and proper maintenance. At

33

**The village street returned to normal in 1923. Next to the pub is Malthouse Farm and the black and white facade of Roe Cottages can be seen behind the trees.**

**The southern end of the parish of Piddinghoe in 1928.**

last, in July 1923, work was finished and the village street became once again a haven for horses and people.

Coinciding in time with work on the road were extensive developments at the coastal end of the parish. In 1920 the electoral roll included two names from Peacehaven and fourteen from Friar's Bay. The 1922 figures were twenty nine and eighteen which, by 1925, had risen to 700 and forty three respectively. In 1929 the total was 1,436, and a separate parish of Peacehaven was formed, occupying approximately half the original parish of Piddinghoe. The 'garden city' of Peacehaven was officially opened in 1922, and by 1924, from the hills above the village, Piddinghoers could look down in the dusk of evening on this sprawling, scattered community twinkling with light, something for which their village would have to wait another fifteen years.

The speed of development along the coast reached its peak in 1928, and then came the Depression. Within three years the Peacehaven Estate Company would go into liquidation, its assets sold to the Saltdean Estate Company.

The village also had some new houses, the first of the century. In 1928 Thomas Colgate, the principal landowner, built himself a home, Brickyard House, on his old Whiting Works site. At about the same time the rural district council put up a pair of semi-detached houses out on the Newhaven road, and an ex-army hut nearby was upgraded to a bungalow.

The development of Peacehaven affected the parish in ways other than by its physical impact on the landscape. In addition to jobs, it later provided modern homes for a few villagers, but its major impact was felt by the school. In the summer of 1924 Phyllis Ives, aged six, was the first child to be admitted from the new town of Peacehaven. In May 1925 came what amounted to an invasion. At the beginning of the month there were thirty five pupils on the roll; by 8 June eighteen from Peacehaven had been added, a fifty percent increase in five weeks. On one day alone came six from three families, ages ranging from thirteen to six. The headmistress, Mrs Jane Muir, lived in Peacehaven so well understood the lives of her new charges, but the difficulties of absorbing so many new pupils in such a short period were formidable. Another seven were admitted in the autumn term. By the end of July 1926, however, all eighteen had left, the majority to go to the 'old tin hut' which was the first Peacehaven school. Yet, for the rest of its life, the village school would always have a few children from Peacehaven on its books.

St John's Church too was affected by the arrival of all these people into its parish. In 1924 the parochial church council had three members from the 'old' parish and three from Peacehaven. Even after a new church was built, brides and grooms clearly favoured St John's for during this decade, in twenty one of the forty two marriages solemnised there, either one or both of the contracting parties came from Peacehaven.

The parish council had to adapt even more vigorously than its ecclesiastical counterpart. The original five members were increased first to eleven and then to fifteen. After the 11 April 1925 election thirteen of the new councillors lived in Peacehaven and only two in Piddinghoe.

The number of people in the parish, excluding Peacehaven, was almost static, but there were significant changes in the nature of the population. The overall family size continued to fall, resulting in fewer school pupils and the consequent removal of the third teacher, Miss Maud Bennett, in 1921.The number of young adults, however, increased. In 1925 Mrs Elizabeth Penfold had eleven of her seventeen children still living in the parish, seven married and four single. Unsurprisingly the church witnessed twice as many marriages in this decade as in the previous one, excluding those living in Peacehaven.

With so many young adults at home, living space in the cottages was at a premium. At Malthouse, the Alces first solved the problem by sending three of the children to sleep in a cottage over the road, then decided to rebuild their house. Children from large families quite often found themselves sent to sleep elsewhere. One elderly resident remarked quite recently: 'I don't reckon there was a house I hadn't slept in when I was a child'.

Occupations at this time were broadly similar to those in previous decades. Some sixty percent of the men still worked on the land, although labourers of all kinds found jobs increasingly hard to come by, with little security of employment. After leaving the army, Dick Alce of

**Dick Moore ploughing for the Durrants at Townsend Farm in 1927.**

Malthouse Farm had six jobs before finding a steady one as a milkman for Mr Thompsett at Court House Farm. Fortunately the increasing popularity of the railway and ferries brought more jobs to Newhaven while Peacehaven was the mecca for all the building trades. A few men were also still employed by the Lower Ouse Navigation Board and in clay-digging. The majority of women continued in domestic service, a few locally, others in private houses, schools, hotels and boarding houses in nearby towns.

Young Olive Paddy, after her experience of being a tweeny in Lewes was pleased to join her cousin Dorothy Boyle who was working for Mr Durrant at Townsend Farm. A typical day for Olive, pictured right, began at 5.30am, moving swiftly to milking, delivering in Newhaven and back to wash the cans, only to repeat the sequence in the afternoon. Customers left a covered jug to receive the milk, and expected two deliveries a day, Christmas included. Other jobs such as hoeing, planting or cleaning harness had to be fitted in whenever possible. Summer evenings brought the chance to earn an extra 7d (2½p) an hour weeding; Olive bought her first watch with her 'thistle' money.

Nationwide, farming had a brief period of prosperity from 1918 until about 1922 when normal trading resumed and there were once again large-scale imports of meat and grain. Farmers were then urged to switch to livestock, especially dairy cows, in order to benefit from the cheap cereal prices. The government, concerned about standards of hygiene in the dairy industry,

**A couple of calves in the yard behind Malthouse Farm**

required local councils to supply information for a register of 'farms and other premises used as dairies' and Chailey Rural District Council made this return on 30 June 1927:

| | | | |
|---|---|---|---|
| Court House | Luke Thompsett | 2 brick sheds | 27 dairy cows |
| Townsend | Fred Durrant | 2 flint/timber sheds | 10 dairy cows |
| Malthouse | James Alce | 1 flint/corrugated iron shed | 12 dairy cows |
| Lodge* | W and R Atkinson | 3 timber/flint sheds | 33 dairy cows |
| Deans | Nevile Gwynne | 2 flint/brick sheds | 37 dairy cows |

\* i.e. Hoddern, on Lodge Hill

Of the ten cowsheds, only one, at Lodge, was said to be in good order.

Looking after dairy cattle was much more labour-intensive than growing crops. Dick Alce did not have a single day's holiday in four years. As his mother said to him: 'It's like this, my boy, you've got two hands, you can go and get your food, the animals can't and they've got to be fed twice a day, everyday.'

Men employed by the Navigation Board spent much of their time maintaining the river bank. They were familiar figures in their black clothes, their boat often moored at the old Whiting Works part of which had been bought by Every's of Lewes, who decided to ship ore for its Phoenix Ironworks to Piddinghoe, then take it by road to Lewes. The wharf they constructed brought in a variety of vessels, including the topsail schooners *Alert* and *Julia.*

The village lads were fascinated by these tall ships which had sailed

The *Alert* unloading her cargo of pig iron at Every's new wharf.

the open seas. Young Frank Stace, who lived in the first house up Harping Hill opposite the wharf, was one of the first to see any new arrival. He made friends with the cook aboard the *Julia,* which brought iron ore from Groningen in Sweden, and used to take aboard freshly-picked field mushrooms, to the delight of the crew. Other commodities unloaded included wood, granite and steel girders. This activity did not, however, bring any jobs to the village, as the work was done by Every's own labour force.

At the other end of the village the clay working employed more men. Ted Bennett, now foreman, worked with three of his sons, together with Charlie Paddy and his son Jack. The trenches had become a sizable pit, although the digging was still by hand. An engine-driven winch dragged the full trucks up from the pit onto the river bank from where they were tipped into the waiting barge, which was still poled up river on the incoming tide. Change was, however, imminent as in 1929 Eastwoods took over the Lewes Portland Cement Company.

Social life within the parish continued in much the same vein as before, with one important addition – the formation of Piddinghoe Football Club. Soccer had long been the boys' winter sport, but by this time there were so many young men in their late teens and twenties that the parish was able to have its own team, which played in the Lewes and District League. They were kitted out in green and amber stripes and they played on the Hoe, with headquarters in the Royal Oak. In 1923-24 the team won the League Cup and in 1928-29 the First XI won not only the League Cup, but also the Lewes Charity Cup, and the newly-formed Second XI narrowly missed being runners-up in the League. Management of the club was entirely village based.

Fund-raising was a major activity with whist drives in the school, run by 'the ladies', being the main source of income. Astonishingly, in 1929, the club even raised £11 11s 2d (£11.56p) for good causes, including the parish church and school. This public-spirited attitude permeated the play too, players giving up half a day's pay in order not to let the side down and paying their own fares to away matches.

Leisure activities outside the parish became more accessible by the introduction in 1924 of a bus service along the new road. It was part of a circular route linking Newhaven, Lewes and Brighton but the cost limited its use by many of the villagers for the adult fare to Newhaven was 3d(1p) with half price for children and 1s 3d (6p) return to Lewes. Many, therefore, still walked to Newhaven, perhaps to go to the Kinema, or the Cinema de Luxe.

In general terms the school routine continued much as before. Many winters were characterised by 'inclement weather', which particularly affected the attendance of children from the outlying farms. Illness too was prevalent. The school log book for the autumn term 1921 makes chilling reading:

'Friday October 14th: Dorothea Robinson, aged 7, who complained of feeling unwell on Thursday afternoon was sent home at 3.10pm. She died on Saturday October 15th.

Wednesday October 19th : . . . Daisy Clements complained of feeling unwell and was sent home. The District Inspectress of Infectious Diseases visited the school and examined the throats of the 36 children present. Of these children seventeen were found to be suffering from some throat troubles and were told to absent themselves for four days.

Thursday October 20th: Received letter from Sanitary Inspector Groves ordering the closing of the school upon the advice of the Medical Officer for Health. The closing is to be for a period of fourteen days.'

**The pupils of Piddinghoe school in 1928 with headmistress, Mrs Muir, on the left and assistant teacher, Miss Muriel Winter, on the right.** *Photo: Village scrapbook.*

Thursday November 10th: Received a further closing order for another fourteen days. The child, Daisy Clements, died from the effects of scarlet fever.'

The regular events of the school year continued throughout the decade, including the Little Edith Treat. Paying the general school bills frequently presented a problem. In October 1928, for example, their bank book showed a credit balance of £2 10s (£2.50p) but outstanding bills amounted to £20 9s 3d (£20.42½p), some £10 of which had been incurred two years previously. It was agreed to seek the help of the football club in organising a whist drive, but, as usual, the school managers had a whip round there and then, as well as each promising a prize for the whist drive. Landowner Mr Colgate quite often paid some of the bills himself.

Out of school, the village and surrounding hills still provided an adventure playground for the children. Harping Hill in the snow brought extra excitement for the lads. Home-made sledges careered across the hills, round the bushes, up and down the dips – a moonlit night transforming the experience to one boy's idea of heaven. Far removed from this idyll, on the other side of the Atlantic, an event occurred on 24 October 1929 which seemed as unrelated to Piddinghoe as it was distant. Yet Black Tuesday and the Wall Street Crash brought world trade to a near standstill and ushered in the 'Threadbare Thirties'.

# 5

# THE DEPRESSION DECADE

## 1930–39

A world-wide resurgence of unemployment marked the beginning of the decade. By 1933 forty per cent of miners and sixty per cent of shipyard workers were jobless. The Jarrow Crusade of 1936 was but one of many protest marches, but it came to symbolise the desperation of them all. When 200 men marched the 300 miles to London where their MP presenting a petition with 11,572 signatures to the House of Commons they returned home to find that their unemployment pay had been cut, since they had made themselves unavailable for work.

The south-east generally was less badly affected than the rest of the country, with the exception of farming. Prices of produce had fallen all through the Twenties, then, in three years from 1929 plunged down a further thirty-four per cent with a consequent loss of jobs. For those in work, however, it was a time of increasing prosperity and opportunity. Public transport flourished as never before, with bicycles and motorcycles remaining the personal transport of most people, although car ownership reached two million in 1939. On Sundays and Bank Holidays droves of city dwellers fled to the sea and countryside and the railway companies produced booklets extolling the delights of the areas they served.

Piddinghoe had its own guest house and tea garden in the former Brickyard House. It opened for business in 1933 as Kiln Cottage, with fifteen year old Mary Bennett, daughter of Ted, as one of the maids. Four or five years later, when in the ownership of Mrs Baird, it advertised 'bathing from the garden, seven bedrooms, two bathrooms and constant

**Kiln Cottage guest house and tea garden.**

hot water.' The Royal Oak also cashed in on the boom in travelling with an entry in the 1932 Cyclists Touring Club Route Book.

In addition to new businesses, there were also five new houses. The substantial Rose Markie, infilled between Roe Cottages and Pear Tree, was followed by two sets of detached bungalows, one at each end of the village. New they might be but, with the exception of the pair next to White Cottage, these homes, like those in the rest of the parish, had neither electricity nor mains drainage. Eventually, in the second half of 1939, light and power arrived at the southern end of the village enabling Harry and Olive Crooks to operate their Hoe Dairy alongside one of the new bungalows. The rest of the village had to wait. It was 13 December 1940 when the school log recorded: 'Electric light fitted'.

Increasing urbanisation of the countryside around Piddinghoe caused the farmers some problems, but also provided a ready market for milk. Dairy cows were now seen even on some of the chalk pastures. Hoddern also had a large flock of poultry and some pigs. Each of the two smaller village farms ceased work in this decade. Fred Durrant, who had taken over from Albert Evenden in 1918, moved away from Townsend in 1931 and no one worked it as a unit again. The land reverted to Court House

44

and the house was let to the cowman, Charlie Dunk and his wife Alice, née Thompsett. In 1937 Jim Alce of Malthouse retired from farming so his land went back to Court House as well, but he owned the buildings and the house remained his family's home for many more years.

In addition to Kiln Cottage and the Royal Oak, Deans remained a source of domestic, as well as agricultural, employment but in the parish opportunities were limited so the majority of women still went further afield to, for example, Seaford, Rottingdean and Brighton. Men also had to search for work. The Saltdean Estate Company continued building along the coast from Rottingdean to Newhaven and skilled men and labourers were needed there and other sites in the county, but almost entirely on a casual basis. Piddinghoe men found jobs in Newhaven, as they had done throughout the century. The railway and its ferries were busier than ever, with plenty of other craft using the harbour, providing

**Jim Alce, jnr, 'helped' by his sons John and Geoff, haymaking at Malthouse Farm in the 1930s.**

**Ted Bennett at the door of the new mechanical digger at the clay pit.**

land and sea based employment. The roar of the fast Pullman Express boat train, hauled by a 'Schools' class engine, speeding to Newhaven was a familiar sound to all Piddinghoers. Although the line was electrified in 1935, relief trains continued to be pulled by the familiar steam engines for many years.

Within the village, two or three men were still employed by the Navigation Board, work for one or two more being provided, in 1939, by the Crooks' dairy. Across the fields the clay pit was entering its most productive phase, following the mechanisation introduced by Eastwoods. Between 1930 and 1939 the area being dug increased from about eight acres to more than twenty two, employing some five or six men. Ted Bennett was still their foreman, until, on 18 June 1934, at the age of fifty nine, he collapsed and died from a heart attack. He had been home for his dinner and had returned to work where he was discovered, lying on the clay, by his son, Tom. Ted was a gifted, versatile man, known and liked throughout the district as well as in Piddinghoe. He was also a talented artist, as can be seen from his painting of the village by moonlight, which is on the back cover of this book. St John's church was packed for his funeral the following Saturday, the congregation including his widow and eight children, the youngest of whom was twelve years old.

**Ted Bennett.**
*Photo: Village scrapbook*

By the late twenties and early thirties the number of villagers seeking work had risen and there was no way in which Piddinghoe, or even the local area, could meet their needs. The majority were married, and there was a limit to how many in-laws and children could be fitted into a cottage. Thus it was that many of this generation were forced to leave the parish, not necessarily unwillingly since the outside world held an increasing number of attractions, not least electricity. As a result there was a sixteen per cent drop in the population and at the school the numbers fell even more dramatically from thirty three in 1930 to twenty three in 1939.Although there were a few new faces in this decade, the majority of the 'public faces' had been here for some years. Elders of this group were Mus' Penfold and Mus' Latter, as they were called. Mus' Penfold, mother of seventeen and

**Mus' Latter at the Stores with daughter, Mary Brockway, and granddaughter, Mary, in 1927.**
*Photo: Village scrapbook.*

47

postmistress for thirty five years, died in October 1930 aged eighty. She was succeeded at the post office by her second youngest son Percy, who was unmarried and lived at home. Mus' Latter, had been at the Stores since before 1900. Her husband died in 1931, but she ran the shop throughout the decade and beyond.

In June 1939 the area lost one of its great characters with the death of Dan Alce. In his early days Dan was captain of a local shearing gang and later he was judged to be a genius with farm machinery, indeed describing himself once as 'engineer'. He was also a robust singer of the old songs. Sussex author and folk singer, Bob Copper, encapsulated Dan's qualities in a poem entitled *A True Story,* which includes these lines:

*Some years ago, yet not so long*
*That no one could recall,*
*There lived a man in Pidden'ew*
*The like of whom there are but few,*
*He stood six feet five inches tall*
*With shoulders broad and strong.*
. . .
*To work with him would break your heart,*
*Why, he could pitch a fold*
*Or hang and tar a five-bar gate,*
*Without assistance from a mate,*
*Before another man had rolled*
*His sleeves or made a start.*
. . .

Also known across the parish was Nevile Gwynne of Deans, to some as employer, to others as the local squire. He came from a wealthy family, remaining managing director of its engineering firm until his death in 1951. In 1920 he had been awarded the CBE for his work on the Clerot rotary aero engine in the First World War. For thirty years he shared his time between South Kensington and Piddinghoe where he had a large indoor staff in addition to his farm workers. The wedding of his daughter Mary, known as Miss Molly, grey-haired Guide Captain and Sunday School teacher, at St John's on 24 October 1931 was a great village occasion, her Guides lining the path to the church door.

Piddinghoe FC in 1931 with its three trophies. Back row: H Penfold Snr. (linesman), H
Faulkner (treasurer) L Alce, H Funnell, R Alce (secretary), V Hollands (assistant
secretary). Middle row: H Penfold, B Beagley, E Penfold, H Bennett, C Burdett,
J Latter. Front row: A S Boyle, J Penfold, S Chisholm, H Penfold.

Nevile Gwynne's role as local squire involved hosting many parish
events, among them the celebrations to mark the coronation of King
George VI and Queen Elizabeth on 12 May 1937. The 'Pushing
Wheelbarrow Blindfolded 50 yards, Gentlemen Only' probably had
the greatest potential for disaster, although the highest prize for an
individual event – 5s (25p) – went to the winner of the one mile cross
country race. In the evening there was a dance with spot prizes,
admission 6d, to the music of the Kaluan Dance Band.

Regular social activities continued much as they had in the
Twenties. In the first years of the decade the weekly whist drives were
still in aid of the football club which, in 1930-31 had its best season
ever, the first team winning the Lewes District League Cup, the Lewes

49

Charity Cup and the Sussex Junior Cup. Of their Charity Cup 7-3 triumph over Green's Athletic the *Sussex Express* had this to say:

> 'In every department Piddinghoe were superior. Their chief strength was in the forward line, which showed fine cohesion and accuracy of shooting. . . The wing men of both teams played well. A fine display was given by the Piddinghoe goalkeeper . . . A brilliant goal was scored by Chisholm ten minutes later . . .'

Of this winning team, eight lived in the village, four with Penfold fathers, two with Penfold mothers, together with an Alce and a Bennett. The club continued until at least 1933, but players were getting older and some moved away, so there were no more trophies to be displayed in the Royal Oak.

In addition to organising whist drives for the football club, some of the women belonged to the Piddinghoe and Southease Women's Institute, which in 1932, at least, was holding monthly meetings in the parish room. On 1 January that year they held the seventh annual treat for children of the two villages. For some this could have been the first of at least three treats they would be able to attend. At Easter there was a Sunday School Party at Deans when dozens of boiled, coloured eggs were hidden for them to find and on 19 July came, as always, the Little Edith Treat. There were other excitements during the school year as Peggy Pawson, neé Alce, recalls:

> 'When the Southdown Hunt met on the Green we loved to mingle with the hounds and stroke them. One day someone suggested we follow when they left and foolishly about six or eight of us did. We ran off up over the hills after the hunt until we were worn out, then trailed back to school expecting to be punished for playing truant. Someone had an orange and said that if we rubbed it on our palm the stroke from the cane wouldn't hurt so much, so we stood in a queue passing the orange behind us to the next in line. Funny thing is, I don't remember that it hurt, so I don't think Mrs Muir used much force . . .'

As the decade neared its end, the school managers and teachers had more on their minds than school work, treats and truancy. On 17 May the first gas mask drill is recorded in the school log as: 'completed in 2 mins'. More momentously, on the first day of the autumn term came not only some twenty eight Piddinghoe children, but also fifteen evacuees.

These fifteen, together with their mothers, younger brothers and sisters and mothers with toddlers under five, had arrived in the village the week before, mostly from Southwark and Bermondsey. Mrs Chapman, formerly Mrs Cook, had been in charge of the billeting arrangements, canvassing most households whether they could take any evacuees and, if so, how many.. The majority agreed and the afternoon of 2 September saw them all waiting in the school room for their unknown guests. Their apprehension can have been but slight compared to that felt by the London mothers with tired but excited children who had left their homes that morning not knowing where they would be sleeping that night. Up the lane and onto the Green came the coach. One of those mothers, Mrs Bullen, describes their arrival:

> 'We were ushered into a hall where we were given a carrier bag containing a tin of Libby's corned beef, a tin of Carnation evaporated milk and a packet of biscuits. We were soon told that I, my sister-in-law and the six children were to be housed together with a Mrs Bennett of Riverside Cottage . . . The following day we heard, for the first time, the ominous wailing of the air-raid siren . . .'

The Bullens stayed for seven weeks. By that time five other families had already gone. Seven children stayed until nearly Christmas, just one saw the school year through. These were the 'official' evacuees. Two or three others, who came independently to relatives, stayed longer. Until the end of the decade, the parish shared the general experience of what became known as the 'phoney war'. The expected air raids did not come, whereas the blackout did, although this had less impact on Piddinghoe than on neighbouring Newhaven, where they had electricity and street lights. The news on the wireless was not good. Some men joined the Services, but events had not moved as swiftly as had been expected following Prime Minister Neville Chamberlain's wireless announcement on 3 September that, once again, England was at war with Germany.

# 6

# ANOTHER WAR

## 1940–49

Defensive preparations continued to be made both locally and nationally. On 1 January men aged nineteen to twenty seven began to be called up. A week later sugar, butter and bacon were rationed and every household was required to register with a local shop. It was a bitterly cold winter, the school was effectively closed for a week from 29 January because of the deep snow and ice. Mrs Muir struggled over from Peacehaven on four mornings but so few children appeared that, after registration each day they were sent home. On Wednesday rain fell overnight then froze, glazing everything with ice up to an inch thick.

At the end of May however, the 'phoney' war became all too real, as the 'little ships' of Newhaven, became part of the armada which rescued thousands of allied troops from the beaches at Dunkirk. Hospital trains sped up the valley, few on board able to appreciate the beauty of the early summer countryside through which they were passing. By 4 June the evacuation was complete and the German Army occupied the land just across the Channel. The threat of invasion was now imminent and at the beginning of July came the first daylight air raid on the UK. The village children practised their air raid procedures and all too soon this practice was to be put to the test.

The Battle of Britain began in August and the Air Ministry estimated that at its height more than 1,000 German planes were being sent daily over Britain. They were intercepted by the Spitfires and Hurricanes of RAF Fighter Command and battles were fought in the skies all over south-east England. At midday on Sunday, 18 August, seven Nazi Dornier 17s roared up the Ouse Valley machine gunning houses and people. On they went, hedge-hopping over the roofs of Lewes, Burgess Hill, Haywards Heath and on to London and their destination – RAF Kenley. After the war another reason for their run of terror was revealed by the production of brilliantly clear photographs, intended no doubt to aid invasion plans.

By September, when the children returned to school, the blitz of other cities had begun, but the pounding of London continued and air-raid warnings became a way of life. During that autumn term, there were forty seven such warnings in school time, and they did not yet have the indoor Morrison shelter, which later would also serve as a table at the rear of the main room. On 24 and 25 October only nine children out of thirty eight came to school, owing to the severity of night time as well as

**Class of 1940. Back row l to r: Tom Holder, Mary Brockway, Peter Brown, Joy Hierons, Peter Bennett, Kathy Strong, Stan Brown, Mrs Muir, Mrs Chapman. Second row: Molly Dunk, Jean Knight, John Alce, Julia Higgs, Len Alce, Beryl Needham, John Latter, Kathy Long. Third row, seated: Violet Monk, Margaret Higgs, Joan Higgs, Doreen Smart, May Holder. Front row: John Stillwell, Leslie Needham, Sheila Combs, John Combs, Robert Needham, Jimmy Holder, Ann Latter.**

day time raids. Yet Piddinghoe remained unscathed. On 11 December however, it was touched by tragedy. That night Newhaven had its worst raid. Three of the four families killed outright when a single bomb demolished three houses in Folly Fields had close Piddinghoe connections. One, Jo Reed, had attended the village school and was sister to villager Winnie Smart. Jo's thirteen-month old baby died too.

The war in the air intensified in the spring of 1941, when London was again the main target for the Luftwaffe's night raids. On the night of 16 April 500 bombers devastated the capital; on 10 May 550 aircraft killed 1,400 civilians. The Lord Mayor of London established an Air Raid Distress Fund: Chailey Rural District Council sent £558, to which Piddinghoe contributed £16 11s.

Despite all this aerial activity, the only damage reported in the parish in the first four years of the war was at Deans, where, on 20 May 1942, six 16inch by 8inch slates were blown off Chapel Barn roof. It cost 3s 6d (17½p) to replace them. Planes, both British and German, came down in the surrounding parishes of Tarring Neville, Southease and two in Iford, but again, none in Piddinghoe.

Meanwhile, the village and Hoddern Farm were engulfed by the army. Two gun batteries appeared, one alongside the now disused clay pit, the other at Hoddern. The former was equipped with a Bofers gun and two machine guns mounted in a revolving turret, manned by about twenty Canadian soldiers. To the local boys the camps's chief attraction was as a source of untold culinary delights, such as treacle pudding, and even tins of jam to take home. At Hoddern there were five or six big anti-aircraft guns and when they opened up the whole village shook. Just down the road towards Newhaven the fields were filled with Americans – a source of chewing-gum and Coco Cola for the lads, nylon stockings for the girls. As well as the guns at Hoddern and the clay pit, others were located in the neighbouring parishes of Tarring Neville and Southease. When they all fired the noise was deafening.

On the wharf at Riverside a large canvas covered REME workshop was set up, together with tanks and tank recovery vehicles. Kiln Cottage was commandeered for billets and Mrs Bennett at Riverside provided lodgings for four Welsh soldiers from Hoddern, one of whom subsequently married her daughter, Rene. Out on the main road, especially under the Lydds on the way to Deans, fifty gallon drums filled with petrol were buried. They were intended to be fired in the case of invasion but the local lads got to them first and drained off the fuel – valuable stuff petrol. Even the pub garden had its stock of petrol bombs.

Men now in their sixties and seventies, looking back on their wartime boyhoods, see them as immensely exciting. Alan Norman, who was staying with his grandparent's at the Old Vicarage, was amazed one morning to find a tank had been winkled into the space between the garden wall and the four elm trees, just feet away on the Green. Temporary bridges were thrown across the river, for trucks and tanks to drive over them, then be rolled back up and away. Tanks were tested on the riverside pastures up towards Southease, and sometimes the lads managed to drive tanks and Bren gun carriers round the village.

Prior to the fateful Dieppe landing in 1942, camouflage covers of chicken wire and sacking concealed some twenty four motor torpedo boats moored in the river by the clay pit. To the boys this was yet one more item in the great adventure playground which was Piddinghoe in the Forties. While their sons revelled in the excitement of it all, their parents were only too aware of the harsher realities of wartime. Some twenty three men and women went into the services, mostly into the navy and army, but three into the air force. Those left at home were sometimes required, sometimes encouraged, to help the war effort in

**Sid and Les Alce of Malthouse Farm were in E Company, Piddinghoe Platoon of the Sussex Volunteer Defence Force, later the Sussex Home Guard.**

**Deans Farmhouse**

various ways. For example, between midday and 8pm on Saturday 31 October and the following Monday, a trickle of men and women would have been seen making their way across the Green to the church room, National Registration Identity Cards in their hands. The men would have been aged between eighteen and sixty, the women between twenty and forty five and all were required to register for fire prevention duties.

An essential part of the war effort was the production of as much home-grown food as possible. A national farm survey (see Appendix II on page 124) was conducted by questionnaire, inspection and interview. With the demise of Townsend and Malthouse, the parish again comprised its three original farms, although each had lost acreage at its seaward end. Hoddern was now the smallest with approximately 230 acres, Court House had some 300 acres and Deans about 350 acres. All three had both arable, a good proportion of which was used for fodder crops, and pasture land. All three kept cattle and poultry but in terms of physical landscape and economic outcomes there were significant contrasts.

Overall Deans had all the advantages including better land and the capital to manage it well. Nevile Gwynne employed thirteen full-time farm staff, as well as five part-timers. Court House had good pasture land out on the Brooks, but the rest of the farm could have been more productive, which is not surprising since Luke Thompsett, a tenant farmer, was now elderly and had only three employees. At Hoddern, Bill and Bob Atkinson had the poorest physical conditions of the three farms, three quarters of their land being designated fair/bad. Although owner-occupiers, they too were getting on in years and employed only four men. At about this time they amalgamated with Cornford's Dairy, selling milk under that name.

From November 1939 until January 1940, a land girl, Pauline Hockney, working at Deans, kept a diary. Although principally concerned with the minutiae of her daily activities, especially the great difficulty she usually had in starting her tractor on these cold winter mornings, her account illuminates life both in the house and on the farm. The 1941 survey referred to brookland at Deans which had been flooded by sea-water two years previously, but which was being limed. This was one of the jobs which Pauline was given to do, one morning carting three loads of basic slag and lime from Chapel Barn out to a field by the river. As part of the war effort high downland was being ploughed for the first time for many years and it caused problems for Pauline:

'I lost two new shares, got a lot of bungs and felt altogether fed-up . . . after lunch I drew the straightest ridge that I have ever done, in spite of the fact that I had to stop every five yards or so to unbung the plough, which continually got trails of brambles round it . . . it took me nearly three hours to make seven short furrows . . .

Locally, the most spectacular event of the war occurred at about 5am on 22 November 1944. In a heavy storm, a barge loaded with more than 180 tons of high explosive, which was being towed down the English Channel, broke free from its tug and struck a landmine under the cliffs just west of Newhaven. The resulting explosion damaged almost every building in the town, people were blown out of their beds and furniture, glass and ceilings sent crashing down on them. Amazingly, only one person was killed, a naval rating, crushed by a falling wall, but hundreds were injured. The force of the explosion was so great that buildings were damaged in all the surrounding villages. In Piddinghoe virtually every building suffered and scarcely a ceiling survived.

Just six months later, on 8 May 1945, came peace – in Europe at least. Victory in Europe, VE day, was declared a national holiday, and in Piddinghoe the children celebrated in the afternoon in true Little Edith Treat style. First came games and races on the Hoe, after Charlie Dunk had moved the cows and other dads had cleared the cow pats, followed, in the school, by as good a tea as rations would allow. In the evening the grown-ups let their hair down at a dance, also in the school.

Overall numbers in the parish remained much as in the thirties. On the electoral roll now, however, came the first evidence of newcomers, a few people who were not farm workers, nor apparently related to

**Piddinghoe FC junior team with the cup the side won in 1948. Back row: David Smart, Rex Dunstall, Billy Dorking, Peter Heaseman, Peter Warren, Johnnie Latter. Front row: Johnnie Paddy, Keith Davey, Billy Boniface and John Smart.**

Piddinghoers. There were fewer baptisms, marriages and burials than in the Thirties, but Peacehaven people clearly still favoured taking their marriage vows in Piddinghoe, since, of the thirty four weddings, eighteen had Peacehaven addresses including Bob Copper's bride Joan, one was from Newhaven and only fifteen from Piddinghoe.

The church registers also give the first clear evidence that, working on the land was now a minority occupation, although this was partly the result of the war. Jobs mentioned divided roughly into one third farming, one third armed services and one third all else, the latter including a banker, although it must be admitted he was a temporary resident. Despite the reduction in numbers of agricultural workers this was still very much a farming parish. In September 1946, the vicar, the Reverend Harries wrote in the parish magazine:

'In this number I ought to tell you the date of the Harvest Thanksgiving, but I cannot do so until we know when the harvest will be gathered in. It's all right if you live in a town to have a fixed date for every year. We who live in the country are much closer to reality, and we cannot sing "All is safely gathered in" when we see the fields full of stooks waiting for the weather to ease up so that they may be stacked. As soon as ever we can see the end in sight, we'll arrange our Harvest Thanksgiving. As usual on that day we shall give our alms to the Royal Agricultural Benevolent Institution, which helps farmers and their families who have fallen on hard times. I am afraid this year will have added considerably to their numbers.'

At this time it was becoming clear how much the war had cost Britain, not just financially, but in terms of the whole economy. The 'Austerity Years' had begun. Rationing became even more rigorous leading to a Black Market in anything which could fall off a lorry, including petrol. The General Election of 1945 brought a Labour Government to power, which launched a huge reform programme of which the National Health Service might have been considered the most radical.

Change came locally on many fronts, the first as the result of a pre-War government initiative offering grant aid to improve the stock of rural housing. Construction started on the 'twelve working-class dwellings' for which Chailey Rural District Council had sought tenders

**Nos 1-6 Brookside Cottages. To the left is Townsend Cottage, newly painted and renamed Huntwick.**

in 1938. The council bought the field next to Townsend Cottage, formerly part of that farm, and employed Bannisters of Newhaven to build three pairs of semi-detached houses fronting The Street and a block of four and two bungalows on the other side of the field, backing on to the Hoe. Each of the houses cost the council £1,432; each bungalow £1046.

Early in 1946, Jimmie and Phoebe Combs, long-time residents of the village, walked the few yards across The Street from their home 2 Roe Cottages, to be ceremoniously given the key to 1 Brookside Cottages. As the houses were completed so tenants moved in, all but one of the other eleven properties going to parish residents, the remaining one to a family being rehoused from a Nissen hut in neighbouring Telscombe. Some of the places vacated were quickly bought and modernised, others were re-let for a while.

Two of the three parish farmers retired in this period. After nearly forty years at Court House Farm, the Thompsetts retired to Brookside, being replaced by Dick and Phyllis Masters. After some twenty five years at Hoddern, Bill Atkinson died in about 1948 and his brother Bill retired the following year, selling to the Wyers.

It was also all change at the school. In March 1946, Mrs Sampford married Nelson Hills, son of Mrs Hills of the Old Vicarage who had been school caretaker since 1929, and in September the headmistress, Mrs Muir retired from a post she had held for close on twenty-one years. Within three months came an even greater upheaval. That which had been discussed as long ago as 1926 came to pass – all the senior pupils were transferred to Newhaven. On the morning of 14 January 1947, only infants and juniors were waiting on

The school building in 1948.

the Green for the sound of the bell. The seniors' journey to Newhaven was, for the first week, made in spring-like weather. Then, on 23 January the thermometer plunged below freezing and stayed there, with record low temperatures and plenty of snow, until March. To these arctic conditions came the new head teacher of Piddinghoe School, Miss Jo Jenner, Mrs Hills jnr having been transferred to another school. There were now eighteen pupils aged five to eleven.

Eighteen months later the diocesan inspector expressed his approval in glowing terms:

> It was a real delight to pay a visit to this very small school. The whole tone and atmosphere, as well as the interior of the building was bright and cheerful, and the children were happy and well behaved.'

In November 1949 Nevile Gwynne visited the school, in his capacity as chairman of the managers, to open the canteen. The need for one had been identified in 1944. Two years later an official from the county council's Education Committee came to see about it. Three and a half years later school dinners were served for the first time. They were cooked in Newhaven and brought in canisters, leaving just serving and washing up to be done at Piddinghoe. All that time had been taken in converting the back lobby into a simple kitchen.

**The WI choir in rehearsal in 1948.**

Kiln Cottage and the Women's Institute both resumed their activities. Mrs Baird at Kiln had looked after soldiers billeted with her in the war years, some of them from the Free French army. The WI was re-formed in 1947 by Lady Castle Steward at the behest of one of the newcomers, Mrs Annie Clowes. Some twenty to thirty members held their meetings in the parish room, establishing a tradition which, with only an occasional change of venue, would continue for a good many years.

The post-war years brought problems for Martyn Harries at St John's. The shaking the building had suffered on 22 November 1944 had resulted in all the roof tiles having to be re-placed and now his congregation was much smaller there was a deficit in funds for the payment of the diocesan contribution.

Work did not resume at the clay pit. With the departure of the soldiers, the empty pit stood silent, its reddy-brown lunar landscape abandoned and forlorn. It had, however, been gradually filling with water ever since the pumps were stilled before the war. By about 1948, one or two intrepid yachtsmen began to sail their boats there – forerunners of the many who were to follow.

# 7

# THE PARISH HAS PLANS

## 1950–59

In the early Fifties it seemed that austerity would never end, especially with regard to food. In an effort to improve public morale the 1951 Festival of Britain was devised, a symbol of good times ahead, and more than eight and a half million people flocked to the South Bank, glorying in this vision of a new life. A setback followed all too quickly with the death of King George VI at the age of fifty-six, in February 1952. Monarchy had been thrust upon him by the abdication of his brother but he earned the affection of the nation during the war and there was genuine sadness at his premature death. However, the Coronation, in June 1953, of his elder daughter Elizabeth, provided not only a cause for celebration and street parties galore, but a phenomenal boost in the sale of television sets.

By the end of the decade, two thirds of the adult population owned one, watching 'the box' on average, twelve and a half hours a week. ITV came on air in September 1955. Homes had labour-saving devices such as toasters and electric kettles, standing on wipe-clean formica work surfaces. ERNIE picked out the first £1,000 premium bond winner, a Hovercraft crossed the English Channel, Sputnik I circled the earth and Lunik II reached the moon. Work was plentiful, even for the unskilled. Small family cars found plenty of buyers, and two week paid holidays kept guest houses and holiday camps busy all summer. Teenagers wearing blue jeans met in coffee bars with jukeboxes. Some became Teddy Boys, with Edwardian-style clothes and Brylcreemed hair.

**The creek and the saltings in the early 1950s with the derelict tug Southerham and the gleaming white hull of a newcomer's craft.**

Piddinghoe seemed far removed from this world, but it was on hand in nearby towns, especially Brighton, which had long been at the forefront of fashion. Even in the parish, however, concern for the young and leisure facilities for one and all were topics of the moment in 1950.

The future of the school was a matter of concern. Could it survive with so few pupils ? There were also worries about the Hoe, which had recently changed hands, and the parish room which had clearly seen better days. For how much longer would the Hoe be available for cricket, fetes and other outdoor activities? If the school went and the parish room, where could indoor social events be held ?

The school re-opened after Christmas 1949 with eighteen children on the roll and everything going well. Ascension Day 1950 incorporated an innovation, no doubt related to the 'canteen'. A service was held in church as usual, but before being dismissed for the rest of the day, the children experienced the novelty of breakfast in school, which happened again the next year. Little Edith's Day 1950 was also unusual. There was the traditional Treat in the afternoon with its time-honoured pattern of games, tea, a present and a scramble for silver coins, thrown up in the air by the vicar, but in the morning the school had endured a Diocesan Inspection, an occasion as much feared by the pupils as it had been by their parents before them. They need not have worried, for when the inspector's report arrived it was as glowing as had been the last one, ending with the words:

'The school has been made a happy family. It is to be hoped that it will long continue its useful work in the village.'

Nevertheless the threat of closure was still in the air. In the event, the school continued its 'useful work' throughout 1951. In June, the vicar

**The last school photograph with Mrs Hills, the vicar Martyn Harries and head teacher Josephine Jenner on the back row. In the class of 1951 are, standing, l to r: Paddy Boyle, Michael Warren, Trevor Fennell, Sheila Jackman, Chloe Boyle, Richard Mullarkey, Malcolm Cannings, Brian Smart, Pat Boyle. Seated: Tom Boyle, Yvonne Holder, Audrey Long, Jasmine Eager, Marion Penfold, Betty Stace, June Fairbrother and Peter Stace.**

brought a man to measure up for the areas to be painted, which must have seemed a good omen for its continuance. Not so, it closed a year later. The much larger Newhaven schools to which the children were transferred in the autumn came as quite a culture shock, occasioning as one recalls, the oft-repeated phrase, 'You're not in Piddinghoe now, you know.' They knew all right.

For much of the century games had been played on the Hoe although its main function was the provision of grazing for cattle belonging to Townsend or Court House Farm. Originally it had been glebe land, but in 1921 it was sold by the Church to Thomas Colgate, who owned all the surrounding land including Court House Farm. By 1946 ownership of the Hoe and Townsend's old cowsheds near its entrance, which had become chalets during the war, was split between three people, each one owning a third of the Hoe and one chalet. At the same time, twelve houses were being built on the adjacent field and agricultural land was being 'developed' with housing nationwide. Clearly, this central open space was under threat and the parish decided to try to buy the Hoe, a view supported by East Sussex County Council, which made it the subject of a Compulsory Purchase Order which became operative on 13 September 1951. Two of the owners were quickly found and compensation sums agreed, the third proved elusive.

Although the parish meeting could obtain a loan for the purchase, it could not raise a rate for its repayment, so it was necessary to re-instate a parish council, the previous one having ceased to function when the parish split from Peacehaven in 1929. Predictably there was opposition. Teddy Port, who had lived in the village all his life, predicted there would be a rise in the rates, which had already doubled since 1939, adding: 'We have lived quite comfortably without a parish council, why do we want it now ? It is not going to benefit the working man, the old age pensioner or the widow and widower.'

The vicar, on the other hand, being himself a member of both Telscombe Parish Council and Chailey Rural District Council, believed it would benefit the village. When the resolution was put a large majority of the sixty people present voted in favour, although there were a number of abstentions. The new council, in June 1955, agreed to purchase the Hoe for the total sum of £300 – purchase price £235, legal costs £65 – and to seek a loan for that amount. In the event only £272 was required, for which a county council mortgage was taken out, involving half yearly repayments of £7 3s 5d (£7.17p) over sixty years.

The small parish room in front of the Old Vicarage was existing on borrowed time. A surveyor had estimated it would cost several hundred pounds to restore it to a reasonable condition and St John's church did not have that amount of money available. The matter was made more urgent by the imminent sale of the school, the only large communal space in the parish. Chailey Rural District Council came to the rescue. It offered to lease to the parish, at a peppercorn rent, a plot of land next to the new council houses, on which could be placed an ex-army hut it owned at Friar's Bay and was willing to sell for £5.

Again Teddy Port led the opposition. 'Any disused Army hut for £5 will be a very ugly sight in our village. The proper value of that is more like 15s not £5,' he said.

'It's worth more than that for firewood,' said a voice from the back of the room.

'That's all it's fit for,' snapped Teddy. 'And the total cost to the village for putting in sanitation, mains water and electricity, is likely to be close on £200.'

However it was decided by a large majority that the hut should be purchased and the land leased. Dick Masters of Court House and Jon Glennon-Anderson of Deans brought the building in sections over from Friar's Bay and work on its reconstruction began, although, as it was winter, it was restricted to weekends. Come the spring however, things speeded up. By May 1955 the building was taking shape. A ladies' working party had been formed to raise funds for the furnishings, and a committee set up to look after the financial and administrative arrangements. The Ministry of Education confirmed a grant of £100 towards the estimated cost of £300. For this sum the village expected to get an attractive wooden structure on brick foundations, measuring 60ft by 20ft. Inside there would be the main room, 36ft by 20ft, with a stage,

**The village hall that never was.**

two dressing rooms/wcs, a kitchen and a lobby. For the rest of 1956 work continued apace and £67 of the grant was received. Indeed, on 28 March the contents of the old parish room, with the exception of the piano and the wireless, were moved in to the new hall.

In the winter, understandably, things slowed, but they did not pick up that much in the summer. The volunteer labour force was beginning to lose interest, drawn back to jobs needing to be done in their own homes and gardens. By October 1958 the Ministry of Education had to be told that the project was in abeyance, through lack of voluntary labour, although the building was well advanced. What had begun with such enthusiasm ended up leaving the village with an untidy building site. The parish was faced with the choice of either having the building completed by a contractor, or demolished and the site cleared. It decided to cut its losses and sell the building, making it a condition that the purchaser cleared the ground. A buyer came forward, paid £50 and removed the hut. More than two years later the parish council was still trying to get the site cleared of rubbish.

The village hall saga had begun in 1953, the year of the Coronation when, on 2 June, celebrations had been held the length and breadth of the land. In Piddinghoe a raffle raised £15 which provided a Coronation mug filled with sweets for each child, and a small prize for every entrant in the afternoon's races, together with lemonade and ice cream. Various other fund-raising activities, including whist drives and a dance at Northease School, raised enough money for a Coronation party at the Royal Oak and later an outing to London to see the lights. Two coach-loads of Piddinghoers, adults and children, set off from the village, excited at the prospect of seeing for themselves what some would recognise from television, but others had only heard about.

Two years later, in 1955 the school building had finally been converted to a house, bringing a new family into the village, but leaving the parish with no meeting place except the Royal Oak, which now housed the WI and the vicar's confirmation classes as well as its usual clients. Meanwhile three new properties had been completed, the only ones this decade.

The school in the 1980s, thirty years after it was converted to a house. *Photo: Village scrapbook.*

Percy Willis, who had owned the field on the other side of the lane from the shop since 1942 and had a holiday home there in the form of a small wooden house, decided to build his own dream house on the site. Between 1952 and 1954, with professional help from a carpenter, bricklayer and plasterer, this former London Transport Board engineer built himself a three bedroom tile-hung detached house and called it Tacolstone after

**The Thames sailing barge *Thetis*, moored in the creek, was the Way family's home for nine years.**

the Norfolk village in which his father-in-law lived. Diagonally across The Street, Chailey Rural District Council compulsorily purchased part of a field belonging to Court House Farm and built two semi-detached houses, which became Purnell Cottages. They were completed in 1952 and their first tenants were long-established Piddinghoe families.

Percy Willis was the first 'outsider' to come to live in the village, in that he was neither related to anyone here, nor worked here. One or two more came in the 1940s but the Fifties witnessed a speeding up of this process. The 1951 census provided something of an outline snapshot of the parish, since some information about housing was included for the first time. The 214 people of the parish lived in sixty three households, corresponding to the sixty three 'structurally separate' dwellings. Of these dwellings, thirteen belonged to Deans and Hoddern, although a few of their tenants stayed for many years, many were short-term. The remaining fifty houses were in the village, only five of which were occupied by newcomers. By the end of the decade, excluding Hoddern and Deans farm workers, some thirty 'new' single people or families had bought, or were renting, properties, together with three who arrived in, and remained resident on, their boats. Some of these early incomers stayed but a short time, others are still in the village.

Despite these 'new' people, overall numbers in the parish fell eight per cent over the decade. The electoral roll was at its lowest in 1956. It was a time of transition. The children of the 'old' families had to move out in search of work and the newcomers tended to be single people or couples with few or no children. Among their number were lawyers, teachers, bank employees and the retired.

The village shop contributed more than its fair share of newcomers over the decade. Jack and Dolly Latter's retirement in 1953 severed a family connection which went back at least to 1866. In contrast to this impressive family stability, between 1953 and 1959, customers had to adjust, in quick succession, to four different shopkeepers. They are remembered as a varied group, one or two not able to cope, the others bright , lively and competent, but clearly Piddinghoe was not for them.

Although in 1952 agricultural workers comprised only twenty three per cent of the total parish workforce, all three farms were in business. Cereal growing was still important in Piddinghoe, compared to other Ouse Valley parishes, but it only accounted for some twenty per cent of the agricultural acreage. Fodder crops were much more widely grown to feed the cows, some of which still meandered along The Street on their way to and from milking. Although two fields bordering The Street were now built on, others brought the presence of the countryside right into the village. Completely absent from these, and all other fields, were sheep, which at the beginning of the century had been the mainstay of the economy. Something like a third of the traditional sheep pastures were lost to the building of Peacehaven, and that which remained was almost entirely encompassed by town houses. Dogs from the towns brought an end, albeit temporarily, to sheep on the Piddinghoe hills.

By 1951, all three farms had changed hands in under five years, the last being Deans. Nevile Gwynne, still very active aged eighty two years, was injured in an accident in one of his cowsheds on 9 July 1951 and died twelve days later in hospital. In September the following year Jonathan and Jacqueline Glennon-Anderson, from Steyning, bought what had, by then, become Deans Place Farm and its five cottages; Nevile's daughter, 'Miss Molly' retaining Halcombe. Deans Farm Cottages, 113, 114, and 115 The Street, were sold to private buyers, so effectively severing the link between the farm and the village.

Like his predecessor at Deans, Jon Glennon-Anderson had outside interests, but also actively farmed the land, although replacing the Gwynne Jerseys with his own Guernseys. He also took over something of Nevile Gwynne's role as unofficial squire becoming the first chairman of the new parish council. Then, as now, the council had five members and a clerk. In terms of a balance between established villagers and newcomers, this first group included two of the former, Horace Faulkner of the Royal Oak and Harry Crooks of the Hoe Dairy, and four newcomers – a proportion which was maintained to the end of the decade.

From 1957, the road from Newhaven brought a new group of people to the village on a regular basis, members of Newhaven and Seaford Sailing Club, which from that date, leased the Pond, formerly the clay pit, from the cement company which still owned it, for an annual fee of £5. And in the summer of 1959, according to the parish council, all too many people branched off the A275 and drove through the village in motor vehicles, including coaches, the drivers putting themselves and the residents in danger. However its request for road signs at the two junctions of the narrow road through the village with the A275 was refused as was yet another plea for a footpath to the cemetery.

Piddinghoe's days as a largely self-contained farming village were at an end.

# 8

# DAYS OF DEVELOPMENT

## 1960–69

The Sixties was the time of Carnaby Street, mini-skirts, the Beatles, Rolling Stones and free love. The Hippy Movement reached its peak in the summer of 1967, its slogan 'make love not war' a protest against the war in Vietnam. For many, especially the young, it was an age of affluence – money to spend and a vast range of goods and services to spend it on. Supermarkets opened on the High Streets and previously unheard-of foods appeared on the counters of an increasing number of delicatessens. By 1965 a million Minis were on the road, including the new motorways, and jet aircraft made foreign travel more accessible. But many were excluded from this glitzy world. In 1967 there were 1.8 million dwellings in England and Wales deemed unfit for habitation. Slum-dwellers, already moved to the new tower blocks, found they had exchanged old, cramped conditions, for modern, lonely ones. Some environmental hazards were dramatically life-threatening: in London in December 1962, three days of smog caused sixty deaths; in Aberfan in 1966, a 116 children and twenty-eight adults died, buried in a school next to an unstable coal-tip.

In contrast to these mean conditions, technology was advancing swiftly, most spectacularly in space, from man's first orbit of the earth in 1961 to Neil Armstrong's 'one small step' onto the moon in 1969. The growth of television ensured that more people than ever before shared in the drama of such events, the solemnity of great state occasions, or the latest episode of *Coronation Street*. Even Piddinghoe could not escape the intrusion of this wider world, and not only on its television screens.

**New houses built in the Sixties in Brookside and, below, in Shepherd's Close, a
development named after its builder, pictured in the 1980s.** *Photos: Village scrapbook*

In the village it was a decade of quite tumultuous change. There was an explosion of house-building; an influx of new people to the church, pub and shop, as well as the new properties, together with developments along the riverside, on the Hoe and to a lesser extent at the former clay pit, now known as the Pond. In the wider parish, the three farms maintained their established patterns of activity, although personnel changed. After thirteen years at Deans Jonathan Glennon-Anderson moved away, selling to Mike Bamber, a millionaire property dealer and a one-time chairman of Brighton and Hove Albion Football Club. The Wyer family continued at Hoddern but change came to Court House. In 1969 Dick Masters gave way to his son Bill, whose wife Mary was a granddaughter of Harry Carr, who had been at Court House then Deans in the first twenty years of the century.

A necessary prelude to any house development in the village was the provision of mains drainage. Chailey submitted a £21,268 scheme to the government for approval in December 1960. Eighteen months later, contractor's huts appeared in a field next to Brookside, later the site of a pumping station. Two years later the contractors were promising to 'reinstate' the Green and tidy up the rest of the village, 'once the last few houses have been connected'. A side benefit of this operation was that they also agreed to remove the last remains of the failed village hall venture – three years after the building itself had been cleared and eight years after the start of the ill-fated project. This site had been leased from Chailey, it being part of land that council had bought for housing. When, in the early Sixties, Chailey came to plan the addition of seven more council houses to Brookside, it realised that it would be helpful if it could also have the small piece of the Hoe that extended into the plot. The parish council agreed to the sale, thereby acquiring sufficient money to pay off the mortgage taken out ten years earlier for the purchase of the whole of the Hoe.

In addition to the Brookside development, thirteen properties were built for private sale with others nearing completion. Rarely was the village free from the noise and dust of building or lorries delivering everything from bricks to boilers. The houses for sale were mostly clustered in

**Part of Court Farm Close, pictured in the 1980s.**
*Photo: Village scrapbook.*

small groups between older properties and the development of Court Farm Close meant that throughout its length The Street was now fenced in by houses, to which the fields were merely a backdrop, symbolising the final separation of the village from its farming environment and inheritance. Court House Farm's large barn, fronting The Street, was sold, together with three adjacent cottages, in which local people had always lived. The barn became a fine house and the cottages were let, usually to short-term University of Sussex staff, some from the USA., Canada or Australia. In 1966, at the height of these new developments, the whole of the Sussex Downs, including Piddinghoe parish, was designated an Area of Outstanding Natural Beauty. Thereafter, all planning policies and decisions had to take the ANOB designation into account.

Between 1961 and 1971 the number of houses in the parish increased from sixty nine to eighty nine and the overall population from 197 to 233. At the beginning of the century almost the same number had lived in the parish, but in half the number of houses. By the end of the Sixties

76

The village looking north. On the left are Deans Farm Cottages; in the centre 1-5 Blythe Cottages; and Old Cottage is on the right. In the background is Harping Hill with its copse of trees.

almost twice as many village houses were lived in by newcomers as by villagers, more than half of the latter in Brookside and Purnell Cottages. The arrival, over a relatively short time, of so many people, mostly from urban areas, was viewed with some apprehension by existing villagers. Mollie Kemp, a 1967 newcomer, found there was a lot to learn:

'Having lived all our lives in a town, we found the country ways were very different from ours, and we certainly had a lot to learn . . . We were invited to the Harvest Supper, a new and delightful experience for us, but one over which we made our first mistake.

'We were in the shop the next morning, discussing the events of the previous evening, and Norman innocently remarked that as the ladies had worked so hard in preparing such a sumptuous repast he had felt that he should have offered to help with the washing up afterwards. Replies to this were surprising and devastating. "Do you think we don't know how to do our job? You people who come from the towns think country folk can't do anything".

'We felt quite deflated. Definitely we had a lot to learn. However, gradually we merged into rural life, and became part of it.'

But did they? Certainly they, and others, came to feel at home in their vision of rural life and some made significant contributions to it. This

77

was not, however, the rural life previously experienced by the villagers. There was not only massive change to the physical environment as they knew it, but, perhaps even more importantly, a major upheaval in its social structure too. The attitudes of some newcomers were not always helpful, as evidenced one day in the shop.

Male ex-army newcomer, heartily, to fellow customer:

'And what do you think of our lovely little village then ?'

Hurriedly the shopkeeper explained that the woman had lived in the village all her life, as had her parents before her. This incident is remembered as clearly now as the day when it happened. Generally speaking the newcomers were wealthier, more confident and more articulate than the villagers. They tended to speak up at meetings, and complain if things were not to their liking. A few, having chosen to live in a village through which cows plodded and plopped every day, were keen to 'improve' it, but then, they were often the ones who moved on before too long.

The church underwent a change of direction early in the decade. Martyn Harries, who was also Rural Dean and a canon of Chichester Cathedral, was not in good health and in 1962 became seriously ill, so decided to resign his joint living of Telscombe with Piddinghoe. However, in the December issue of the parish magazine he wrote that he felt so much better 'that I find it hard to believe that I have reached the end of the road,' adding that he was looking forward to the golden jubilee of his ordination, to be celebrated on 21 December by Sung Eucharist in St John's Church, in the presence of many local clerics including the Bishop of Lewes. Having read that their vicar felt so much better the congregation arriving that morning was all the more shocked to learn that he had died the previous night. The celebration, to which he had so looked forward, became his Requiem Mass. On the day of the burial of his ashes in Telscombe churchyard, a snow plough was needed to clear the road of 18 inches of snow.

The Reverend Derek Payne, who succeeded to the living was, in many ways, totally unlike his predecessor. However, he met at least two of Squire Ambrose Gorham's wishes regarding the appointment of a vicar which he expressed in his will when he left his Telscombe lands and church patronage to Brighton Corporation:

'I prefer that the Corporation shall prefer a man who is a sportsman and not a total abstainer from alcohol and tobacco.'

Derek Payne had played cricket for Northamptonshire and batted and kept wicket for the Church of England XI. He was happy to adjourn to the Royal Oak after choir practice.

The new vicar's first winter was the coldest since 1947. Snow and ice again lasted from Christmas until the beginning of March and for five weeks the Pond became a skating rink, an activity enjoyed by a surprising number of villagers who still had their skates from the cold winters of earlier days. The weather put paid to the church's antiquated heating system, and the organ needed an overhaul. St John's was facing expenditure far in excess of what its relatively small congregation could meet.

Various fund-raising activities were organised, including, on 11 July 1964, a 'Grand Village Fair, with Barbecue and Dance in the evening.' From 1967 to 1969 Telscombe and Piddinghoe joined forces to produce spectacular fairs on the Hoe, to which, in each of the last two years, came some 2,500 visitors. Parish ties bearing Piddinghoe's dolphin crest on a blue, green or maroon background were on sale. They had been designed and supplied by Hugh Rae of Lewes and cost 18s 6d (92½p), five shillings (25p) of which went to the church. They were snapped up, not only locally but by people from as far afield as the USA, Canada, Bahrein and South Africa. Although not as financially successful as the ties, the vicar's willingness to be sponsored, in 1968, for runs scored in the *Church Times* Cricket Cup, must have been one of the more unusual fund-raising activities undertaken at St John's.

The Royal Oak lost a long serving licensee with the retirement, in February 1966, of Horace Faulkner and his wife, Lucy after thirty-six years in which they had seen great change. The young couple who took over the Oak, Eric and Linda Cook, provided food as well as drink and customers began to come from without, as well as within, the parish. One morning a large hole appeared in the flint wall in front of the pub garden. Apparently a lorry had, fortuitously or perhaps accidentally, backed into it during the night. A little more demolition made the gap wide enough for an entrance to a car park, which was soon laid and the rest of the garden turfed to provide an outdoor drinking and eating area.

The village shop also changed hands after ten years during which five shopkeepers had come and gone. Retired grocer Nelson Caplin and his wife, Betty, arrived in 1964. Not only did they regenerate the shop, but Nelson, in particular, became something of a Piddinghoe institution. White-haired, bright-eyed and small in stature, he was quickly into everything.

While building was proceeding at various points along The Street, developments were also taking place along the river. Two houses were built, one on the old Whiting Works site, the other on the old allotments under Church Bank. From 1964 they had the company of boats belonging to the Newhaven Deep Sea Anglers, a club which had been

**The Deep Sea Anglers' moorings and new house on old wharf.** *Photo: Village scrapbook.*

forced to leave Sleepers' Hole in Newhaven where a new marina was being built. The club rented the old wharf wall, which it extended with tubular scaffolding to make moorings for twenty-four boats. No sooner were the boats installed than the news came that the London region of the Youth Hostels Association had plans, in an advanced state, to moor a hostel boat at the saltings. The only relevant group not so far consulted seemed to be the parish council. When members saw the MV *Queenleigh* at Newhaven there was consternation. It had an 'ungainly bus-top structure on its upper deck,' a total lack of a 'marine silhouette' and was 'plain hideous'. Meetings, letters and telephone calls continued from September 1964 through to June the next year when the village decided, by twenty one votes to three with four abstentions, that it was opposed to the establishment of a Youth Hostel in Piddinghoe. That was the last heard of the *Queenleigh*..

Down river, the Newhaven and Seaford Sailing club's use of the Pond was increasing and in 1962 it installed two beach huts there. Three years later a member caused chaos in the village by bringing down the electricity wires with the mast of a boat he was towing.

Over on the Hoe, the shouts of footballers and supporters were heard again, now on Sunday mornings. In 1960 a new club had been formed which had supporters, including its chairman Jim Penfold, from the parish, but the majority of its playing members lived elsewhere. After the Piddinghoe club came Fergusson Radio for a year then British Railways Newhaven FC saw the decade out. There on the touchline every Sunday would be ardent soccer fan, eighty-seven year old Olive Stace, in her wheelchair. And on Saturdays this indomitable grandmother would be taken by her daughter, May Corrie, to the Goldstone ground whenever Brighton and Hove Albion had a home game. They would leave by bus for Newhaven at 12.30pm, catch a train to Hove, walk to the ground, queue for tickets for the stand and, if unlucky, watch the match from the terraces and arrive back in Piddinghoe around 6.30pm.

The football clubs used the chalets at the entrance to the Hoe, formerly Townsend Farm's cowsheds, as changing rooms. By 1967 they were very dilapidated and were gradually being destroyed by children, but three

**Court House Farm barn, converted to High Barn, viewed from Court Farm Close.**
*Photo: Village scrapbook.*

years later plans were afoot to buy them and convert them into a village hall. Renewed calls for a hall had come at a parish meeting in 1964, and it was agreed that the idea should be investigated. Understandably, cynical comments were also heard. 'Oh yes ? We've been here before.' The presence, however, of people with no knowledge of the previous fiasco, meant there was a core of goodwill.

The arrival of Miss Margery Abrahams, purchaser of Court House Barn and its neighbouring cottages, was to prove a decisive financial factor in this latest quest for a hall, which came to fruition in the next decade. She was an exceptional woman who played a full role in village life. Her career, prior to retirement in Piddinghoe, was remarkable, not least because it encompassed two quite different strands. A history graduate from Somerville College Oxford, in 1919 she was invited to work for the Zionist Organisation, and became private secretary to Dr Chaim Weizmann, later to be the first President of Israel. In the mid-Twenties she resigned and changed direction completely. After taking a

Master's Degree in Nutrition (in New York) she went to St Bartholmew's Hospital in London as its first dietician and subsequently had a most distinguished international career in dietetics.

Other newcomers also became involved in parish affairs. As early as 1961 all five members of the parish council were professional or business men, but included the vicar, Martyn Harries, and Dick Masters of Court House Farm. This general pattern continued throughout the decade, although without a representative of the church after 1962 and of the farming community after 1967. The annual meeting at which Dick Masters resigned, was 'stormy' according to the headline in the local paper. Even the reading of the minutes of the previous year's meeting raised noisy protests, including several cries of, 'There should be another election,' and 'I think a lot of jiggery-pokery has been going on,' from one particularly disgruntled inhabitant. The cause of the complaint was the lack of an election in 1966, which was inevitable as only four nominations had been received. They were the existing four councillors who, at their first meeting, co-opted one of their 'friends'. In fact there had not been a contest for election to the parish council since its reinstatement in 1955.

Another bone of contention was the proposal to install a barrier across the river path below the church, 'to preserve it from damage by cars'. Again tempers flared.

'It's been a bridleway for forty years' contended one.

'We want freedom in the village' called several.

After a lengthy discussion, the proposal was defeated by fourteen votes to five.

The final engagement in this Us v Them battle came on 1 May 1969 when ten candidates stood for election for the five council places. Only one of the '67 cohort stood, and he was defeated. Of the five elected, one was a village-born working-class man, and one a woman.

Much of the council's business has a familiar ring – scores of letters to the rural district and the county council on the state of the roads, the verges, the drains, the bus service, abandoned vehicles, speeding traffic through the village and its danger to children. Successes included re-siting the bus shelter which required a new layby; realignment of the junction at the northern end of the village; and, wondrously, the completion of the footpath along the main road to Newhaven, fourteen years and umpteen letters after the request had first been made.

The Hoe was also a major responsibility. In addition to grass cutting and general maintenance, trees were planted and the play area extended. Back in 1957 Harry Crooks had put up swings for the children. In 1968 it was decided to add a sandpit and climbing frame for them and the vicar contributed the profits from the August Flower Festival to this good cause. A year later the sandpit was completed and a Jungle Gym frame installed which would be used by village children for more than twenty years.

Twenty to thirty village women actively supported the WI throughout the decade. Membership was drawn from both newcomers and villagers but even so, 'old' and 'new' tended to sit separately. Until 1966 they could be found on the second Thursday of each month in the club room of the Royal Oak but when the Faulkners left they had to find another venue, which they did, moving to the bungalow behind Malthouse Farm, now called Folly's End. Lady Castle Stewart, who had re-started the Piddinghoe WI, was at its twenty-first anniversary meeting there on 4 February 1968.

# ⑨

# AT LAST – A VILLAGE HALL

## 1970–79

Within six months of the beginning of the Seventies six million working days had been lost to strikes, setting a pattern for the decade. In each of the winters of 1972 and 1973 a State of Emergency was declared, when strikes and overtime bans in essential industries threatened a breakdown in the national power supply. Three day working weeks were introduced to save energy. Throughout the decade, waves of strikes followed each other, involving diverse groups of workers. Countrywide, people became accustomed to disruption and inconvenience. Even *Coronation Street* disappeared from the nation's television screens in 1979, when ITV was forced off the air for five months. The youth culture too reflected a more aggressive attitude to life, as it moved from long haired hippies, via crewcut skinheads to pierced punks.

Doubt rather then aggression characterised two other events of the decade. The new money introduced on Decimalisation Day, 15 February 1971, was regarded with suspicion by all but the very young. People suspected, often quite rightly, that prices rose in the translation, a further fuel to inflation. Two years later, Britain joined the European Economic Community, a referendum in 1975 giving an overwhelming 'yes' to continuing membership. As if in consequence,the following summer brought four months of 'continental' weather, blistering heat and drought, causing severe water shortages. It was particularly disastrous for farmers.

A picture of the village at the beginning of the decade is provided by a Conservation Report on the villages of the Ouse Valley, prepared by

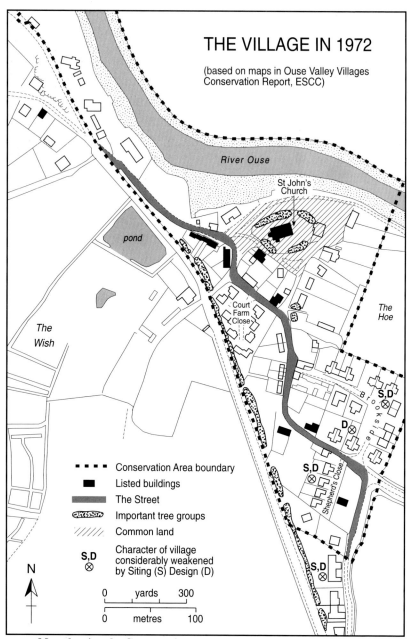

## THE VILLAGE IN 1972

(based on maps in Ouse Valley Villages
Conservation Report, ESCC)

River Ouse

St John's
Church

pond

Court
Farm
Close

The
Hoe

The
Wish

Brookside

S,D

D

Shepherd's Close

S,D

S,D

- - - - Conservation Area boundary
▪ Listed buildings
The Street
Important tree groups
////// Common land

S,D
⊗  Character of village
considerably weakened
by Siting (S) Design (D)

N

| 0 | yards | 300 |
| 0 | metres | 100 |

**Map showing the Conservation Area boundaries and listed buildings.**

86

East Sussex in consultation with Chailey. The Piddinghoe section has these comments from the planners:

'Few buildings of distinction, but overall character warrants conservation.'

'Appearance is much diminished by overhead wires.'

'Numerical balance between old and new now finely drawn.'

'Unfortunately the modern development within the village has not reached the desired standard of layout or detailed design of the dwellings. Some sign of improvement in layout of the most recent.'

This 'most recent' development was Court Farm Close, with its eight properties. Two other village houses were built in the 1970s, one on the wharf and one on Harping Hill, making a total now of ninety nine; and at Deans Farm a third cottage was added to the two above Chapel Barn. This was, however, a tiny development, compared to the transformation of the major land holdings in the parish which took place in the Seventies. After twenty three years the Wyers left Hoddern, selling to Angela and Charles Beeson. The new owners modernised the house and, as he was a racehorse trainer, extended the stabling to take twenty two horses and made a seven furlong training gallop beside the track from the village. By the time they left, they had significantly increased the cultivation of cereals to about half the acreage.

In 1975, Mike Bamber left Deans and the house and outbuildings were bought by Roy Evershed, the land by Peter and John Carr. They also acquired much of Court House Farm, some 200 acres, from their sister and brother-in-law; their uncle Tom taking the Brooklands to be used in conjunction with his farm at Saltdean. Then in 1977, Hoddern Farm came on the market again, and the Carr brothers were able to link together their land at Court House and Deans, Peter and his family moving into the farm house. Such amalgamations were very much the order of the day, small farms being no longer economically viable. After the loss of their lands to Peacehaven, all three Piddinghoe farms were only of the order of 200 to 300 acres. No doubt Harry Carr, who farmed both Court House and Deans in the early years of the century would have been gruffly pleased, as was his wont, to see two of his grandsons back on his

**The grade II listed Hoddern Farm with five period cottages, four with vacant possession and 240 acres was sold before auction for around £400,000 in 1977.**

land. Of his thirteen children, eight of his sons became farmers and three of his daughters married farmers.

With the end of the property boom the population of the parish between 1971 and 1981 rose by only five per cent. In 1978, of the 179 on the electoral roll and living in the village, seventy seven per cent were newcomers who had moved in after 1960. Even among the remaining villagers, none were now farm workers, with the exception of the Masters at Court House Farm, and only six had ever been so. As for the newcomers, a number were retired and for others the village was the place to which they returned after work and in which they would spend at least some of their leisure time. With them came their cars, the proportion of households with two cars rising from eighteen per cent in 1971 to twenty five per cent ten years later when two per cent of households had three or more vehicles..

There was also considerable movement in and out of the village, especially from the new houses. The sixteen properties in Court Farm

Close, Shepherd's Close and the new ones at the southern end of the village, had thirty one different occupants over the decade. Honey Hill, at the southern end, changed hands five times, while three in Court Farm Close and one in Shepherd's Close did so three times.

Developers did not easily give up trying to find somewhere to build. With no large central space now available, they turned their attention to the village fringes. Fifteen houses on a field between the Hoe and the Pond, four on the allotments between Court House Farm and Harping Hill, and a touring caravan site along the river north of Kiln Cottage were all submitted for planning approval and all rejected.

A property which caused considerable concern to villagers was Greenways opposite the church, home of the Penfold family for nearly seventy years. After Elsie Penfold's death in 1970, three unsuccessful attempts were made to develop it. One plan was to put a house and two garages in the garden fronting The Street, another to change it into a tea room and tea garden and a third to build an additional three bedroom house on the site. Meanwhile it stood empty and the garden became a

**South Green, formerly Greenways, home of the Penfold family for at least seventy years.** *Photo: Village scrapbook.*

89

**Derelict cowsheds were quickly converted to the handsome hall, pictured below dressed overall for the Silver Jubilee celebrations, which was formally opened by Mrs Heloise Martin on 26 April 1973.** *Photos: Village scrapbook.*

wilderness, a sad sight to all those who remembered it well cared for and the house teeming with four generations of Penfolds. In 1973 it again became a family home, its name being changed to South Green.

While this was happening, the quest for a village hall was resumed. Miss Abrahams had given a sum of money to the church with a view to building a hall to replace the long-lost parish room, and by May 1970 she was negotiating with Payne and Needham for the purchase of the derelict chalets at the entrance to the Hoe. Nothing came of it and the money was returned to her. However, she retained faith in her idea and turned her attention to the parish council. In July 1971 it called a village meeting which agreed that a working party of four should assess the viability of the project. This was enough for Margery Abrahams. Losing no time at all, she engaged a London firm of architects to provide a schedule for the conversion of the chalets, obtained an estimate of £4,675 for the work from a local firm of builders and bought the chalets for £700. Meanwhile the working party was writing to numerous bodies seeking grant aid, and sending a questionnaire to all villagers to ascertain their level of interest in the proposal.

In July the government grant application was turned down, taking with it a related one from the county council. However the county agreed to apply for a special grant of £2,600, to which it would add £1,300 if the government one succeeded. On this slim hope, work began on clearing the site. Volunteers toiled for the rest of the summer and on 22 September they learned that the grant application had been successful and £3,999 was available. That was the good news, the bad news was that it had to be spent by 31 March the following year which meant that there was only six months in which to convert derelict cowsheds into a hall with a 28ft by 12ft main room, a smaller committee room, full-sized kitchen and two lavatories. To their great credit not only did the volunteers cope with the complexities of the work, but also with the inevitable disagreements which, more than once, threatened to sink the whole enterprise. It was essential to keep everyone on board since, although the grant was the lifesaver, it only covered part of the cost. For some fund-raising became a way of life, the final balance sheet showing that, with bank interest it produced £1,692.65, and the Fayre £600 towards the £7,000 total cost of the project.

Having acquired a hall Piddinghoe lost its shop. In February 1975, Nelson Caplin retired at the age of seventy. Ten years before he had saved the business from near collapse and for a couple of years trade increased, but then stagnated. So ended a business which had been a grocer's shop since 1862, however Nelson and his wife Betty used part of the shop for the post office, which they continued to run into the next decade.

While the villagers were converting cowsheds, along the river the Newhaven Deep Sea Anglers were starting on an engineering project which would occupy them for the best part of twenty years. The club was still renting the old wharf wall, which had been encased in scaffolding to provide more moorings, and had bought the saltings with a view to extending the wharf in that direction. First, however, the saltings had to be built up with tonnes of chalk rubble, then the scaffolding put back to provide temporary moorings for fifteen boats.

A planning application to extend the moorings by 150ft unleashed the pent-up annoyance of many local people at the appearance of what was beginning to be called the 'Fisherman's Wharf'. What the numerous new villagers did not know was that for many a long year there had been nothing on the wharf but a load of old scrap and the saltings, in their natural state, were the 'muddy islands' beloved of village children for half a century. The 150ft extension plan was turned down so the club continued building a massive wall around the saltings, its foundations being 8ft wide, 4ft deep at the front, 2ft deep at the back and descending 8ft below Low Water mark. It was designed by Bob Martin, who lived at Kiln Cottage and was a civil engineer at Newhaven Harbour.

Sporadic complaints about the sea anglers surfaced at parish council meetings. Mostly they were to do with club members' cars obstructing the road at the northern end of the village and turning the wide grassy verge into a mud-bath, but there were also concerns about general untidiness and smoke from bonfires. Overall, however, a truce seems to have been declared, with admiration from some at the scale of the undertaking, all being achieved by voluntary labour.

Piddinghoe church choir in 1971. Back row: Organist 'Jimmie' Combs, Marybud Chignell, Michael Parker, Sam Murray, Janice Hibling, the Reverend Derek Payne. Second row: Peggy Megaw, Nicky Walker, Mollie Hedger. Sitting: Christine Lower, Julie Templeman, David Hibling, Deirdre Lower.

No sooner had the frenzy of fund-raising for the village hall died down, than the church was again in need of repair – £1,650 worth. Fortunately the vicar, Derek Payne, had been immensely successful in building up the size of his congregation, having among other initiatives, instituted an annual pilgrimage service for people from both parishes to give thanks for the Christian Faith. The first was on 21 March 1971 and it was a great occasion. Music from the Ditchling Hand-Bell Group greeted members of the congregation of St John's church as they made their way to the pews. Massed choirs entered, singing the processional hymn *Eternal Father Strong to Save*. At their head was the beautiful cross, recently designed by John Skelton for St Laurence's at Telscombe. It was followed by the Piddinghoe choir robed in green, Telscombe in blue and Newlands School, Seaford, in magenta. Derek Payne was in a purple cope and delivered his sermon from the chancel steps. Sussex cricket captain Mike Griffiths read one of the lessons.

The Piddinghoe choir went from strength to strength in this period and a junior choir was started. Tremendous support for all the church music came from 'Jimmy' Combs who, when he died in 1974, had been the church organist for a record forty eight years. Another long-serving servant of the church was Daisy Paddy. In April 1970 the parochial church council gave her a hymn book and electric kettle to mark her thirty years of looking after the church, ten years with Mrs Hills and a further twenty years on her own, a service she was to continue into the next decade.

It was in 1971 that Piddinghoe had twinning trouble. One Sunday in July the new chairman of the parish council, Norman Kemp, was visited by a reporter who questioned him about the disagreement the village was having with Cleres, near Rouen in France. 'What disagreement?' asked Norman, and so learned of what had already appeared in the French Press, would be on Southern TV in a week, and in the *Sunday Express* within ten days. It appeared that, some eighteen months previously, Derek Payne had visited Cleres, liked what he saw and suggested a twinning arrangement with Piddinghoe. Cleres mayor and council thought this a splendid idea and immediately set about making the necessary arrangements, including naming a new street Rue de Piddinghoe, to please their English friends. They sent a parcel of information and photographs to Piddinghoe, eagerly awaiting a response. They waited, and waited. Four times they wrote, but no reply.

Hurriedly, Norman called the parish council together. The vicar was on holiday. What could it do ? It wrote to Cleres, much regretting what had happened and explaining the situation. The vicar's return did little to solve the mystery. He said that he had given the parcel to the previous chairman – a claim subsequently denied by that chairman, a head teacher, who had left the district – and had assumed the parish council had taken over responsibility for it. Norman and the treasurer, Monty Montague, decided they must go to Cleres and explain in person what had happened. They boarded the 7am ferry from Newhaven, made their way from Dieppe the 75km (50miles) to Cleres and to their surprise found it was a sizable community with more than 1,000 people, shops, an hotel, motor museum and a mayor with an expense account. They were welcomed most warmly but through their minds flitted pictures of Piddinghoe, with its adult population of some 180 people, one small shop, a pub and no public money at all, and they knew that the disparity in size between the two places was just too great for a twinning arrangement to be possible. In September, a village meeting was held to debate the whole issue. It was agreed that Piddinghoe should not twin with Cleres. In his reply to their letter, Dr Layet, Mayor of Cleres, having now visited Piddinghoe himself and found it 'charming', regretted their decision, but understood it.

The vicar had now turned his mind to other fund-raising activities of a sporting nature such as sponsored walks and golf drives. The route of the walks varied each year but was always on downland, extending to Southease when that parish was added to the united benefice in November 1975. The first walk, in 1971, raised the astonishing sum of £511, which was split between two local charities; subsequent efforts going to the maintenance of the churches. The golf drives were run jointly by Rotary and the churches, and involved each contestant hitting a golf ball from Deans over hill, dale, ploughed fields, gorse and barbed wire fences to the rectory at Telscombe. And he had another brainwave in 1971. He said casually to Sheila Redman: 'How about trying a flower festival to raise money – just this year?' so inspiring an event which has featured regularly in the Piddinghoe calendar ever since.

Derek Payne resigned to take up an appointment as chaplain and cricket master at Seaford College, near Petworth in 1976 and was succeeded by the Reverend Geoffrey Holmes. He was the first incumbent since the creation of the united benefice some hundred years previously to live in the village. The diocesan authorities had sold the old rambling rectory at Telscombe because none of the applicants was prepared to live in it, and bought instead Elderberry House, 8 Court Farm Close.

Repairs were soon on the new vicar's agenda, most visibly for the gilded fish weathervane on the shingled round tower of St John's church. It had turned with the wind there since the church was restored in 1882 and gained fame by being referred to by Rudyard Kipling in his poem *Sussex* as a 'begilded dolphin'. It is, in fact, a salmon, modelled on one seen on a fishmonger's slab in Lewes High Street by the man who made it, Edward Blaber. It had rusted on its pivot and had not turned in the wind for some time. When it was removed to be repaired and regilded the metal fish was found to be full of dents and holes made by pellets from the air rifles of generations of Piddinghoe marksmen. In its mouth were two 1936 pennies, inscribed with the names E Alce and J Pellett. Assuming the pennies were new Ted Alce would have been in his thirties and Jim Pellett twenty five when they climbed the tower to put them there.

**The fish vane in close up shows clear evidence of air rifle attack.**

Sports continued on the Hoe, new ones being tug-of-war and tennis. In 1970 a group of young men from the locality, including several from Piddinghoe, formed the Golden Valley Tug-of-War team, reaching the quarter finals of a national contest. For the next few years, on the Spring Bank Holiday at the end of May, they organised successful tug-of-war tournaments on the Hoe. The idea of having a tennis court was put to the test of a village meeting in September 1977. The go-ahead was given, a working party set up, letters were written, events organised and by November the following year £2,250 had been raised and the tennis club formed, its first task being to find the additional £1,500 required to build a court. This it did and the first match was played on the evening of the Summer Fayre, 23 June.

The village fairs of the Seventies were direct descendants of those run jointly with Telscombe in the Sixties. The format was much as before, numerous sideshows and stalls, a silver band and two marquees, one for teas, the other for WI produce and handicrafts and a tombola. Children were able to take leisurely pony rides, bumpy Landrover rides, climb all over a fire engine, or just play on the swings and slides, while their exhausted parents sat in the sun and listened to the band. When the tide

'Anyone for tennis?' Margery Abrahams, suitably dressed for the occasion, cuts the ribbon to open the tennis court. *Photo: Village scrapbook.*

was right, the Deep Sea Anglers provided trips up-river. In the evening, some 100 villagers and helpers would sit down to supper in one of the marquees. In fine weather visitor numbers consistently exceeded 1,000, in 1973 they were estimated to be 1,500. Financially they were very successful. Between 1970 and 1980 a total of £5,000 was raised £2,500 of which went to the village hall fund, £1,050 to the church, £750 to the tennis club and £700 to the parish council.

The WI meetings moved from Folly's End to the new village hall which was used not only by existing groups but also for a programme of activities promoted by the committee. Four of its original ideas are still going strong, three even on the same days of the week – the weekly table tennis and coffee and chat, the monthly supper club and 'interest' evenings.

Piddinghoers know how to celebrate an occasion and on Silver Jubilee Day, 7 June 1977, villagers and visitors alike seemed determined

97

**The pram race sported some rather elderly 'babies', including seventy-two year old postmaster Nelson Caplin in the striped bobble cap.** *Photo: Village scrapbook.*

to have a good time in spite of the Arctic weather. Children exhausted themselves in eleven events in their afternoon of sports and were ready for tea outside the village hall, complete with a Jubilee Cake. On the Hoe the Men of Piddinghoe beat the Piddinghoe Men at cricket and some ninety people had a barbecue supper in the garden of the Malthouse, before a bonfire and dancing on the Hoe, followed by a fancy dress party in the Royal Oak, won, appropriately enough, by Winnie Smart as Britannia.

By 1979, many people were pleased to see the back of the Seventies for generally it had been a troublesome time. Memories of the recent 'winter of discontent' were, however, still fresh, so no quick-fix solution to the nation's ills was expected, which was just as well. The next decade would bring considerable wealth to a few, but greater hardship to many.

# 10

# A MORE SETTLED SCENE

## 1980–89

The Eighties brought contrasts and change, with one powerful linking force, the Prime Minister, Margaret Thatcher. Britain's traditional heavy industries, such as coal and steel, were in steep decline, while computer technology was reducing the workforce in other fields, leading to the highest unemployment figures since the mid-Thirties. Add to this wage claims related to the high inflation, twenty per cent in 1980, and the scene was set for the strikes which continued throughout the the decade, most memorably that of the miners in 1984-85. Violence flared not only on the picket lines, but also on the streets, and most spectacularly in October 1984 when, at the start of the Tory party conference, the IRA attempted to blow up the Grand Hotel on Brighton seafront and the Prime Minister and members of the Cabinet with it.

In contrast this was also the decade of Peace demonstrations, such as the womens' camps at Greenham Common, protesting against the arrival of Cruise missiles at the American airbase. Compassion on a massive scale was energised by pop concerts and records such as Live Aid in 1985, and the first Comic Relief Day in 1989.

In Piddinghoe the Eighties was a period of consolidation and settling down, with fewer new houses, and fewer new people than in either of the previous decades. The village hall moved on from being a novelty to a well-used social asset. The parish became accustomed to having its vicar resident, and many of the social activities of the Seventies continued to be popular. Inevitably there were changes. In April 1983 came the death

99

**Piddinghoe's post office in the early 1980s.** *Photo: Village scrapbook.*

of Margery Abrahams, Piddinghoe's most generous benefactor. Nearly eighteen months later the illness of Nelson Caplin resulted in the closure of the post office. Fortunately for the village, Brenda Cavie was prepared to run a community post office, hours 9am–1pm five days a week, from her home in Brookside. Nelson Caplin died in 1984 and a year later Nelson's Column, a street light bought by public subscription, was switched on by his widow, Betty. In Piddinghoe which, even in the twenty-first century, is still dark, it lights the centre of the village, between his former home and the village hall, where he was so often to be found. By the end of the decade, the village lost its post office for good. Brenda had to resign for personal reasons and no replacement could be found. Clearly Piddinghoe was following the same pattern as so many other small places, its services disappearing, one by one.

Three new houses were built on the site of the former fine 1930s detached house Rosemarkie, renamed Rosemarie by Henry Thompsett. The developer had wanted to put four detached properties there, but was allowed only three by the planning authority. Built in 1984, they still dominate their site, now called Cedarwell Close. A fourth house, finished two years later, was the most unusual ever seen in the village. It was built in the quarry once belonging to, and opposite, the old Whiting Works. From 1960 onwards, successive developers had built larger and more expensive properties, each time taking them further beyond the means of the ordinary people of the parish.

After twelve years of active involvement in village events Harry and Marion Cragg retired from the Royal Oak and were succeeded by Len and Barb Ebbs. They made improvements both inside and outside the pub, supporting village activities cheerfully and generously. Len was also the driving force behind the formation of another Royal Oak football team. In its first season it won Division 1 of the Lewes and District Sunday League, which carried automatic promotion to the Premier Division. Unfortunately better ground facilities were then required, which could not be provided, so the team had to stay in Division 1. Len retired from the trade in 1987, Neville and Sue McEvoy taking over. Almost immediately they introduced a concept new to Piddinghoe – a restaurant, in the former club room which had been the scene of all the celebratory suppers earlier in the century.

Along the river, the remains of the old claypit jetty, deemed to be dangerous, were removed by the Southern Water Authority in the spring of 1984. Had the workmen looked up from their labours, they would have seen, just beyond the church, the Deep Sea Anglers' wharf wall, which had been 'topped-out' that January. In spite of this significant development there was still a great deal to do, and some Piddinghoers were getting a bit tetchy at the time it was taking. On more than one occasion construction stopped completely while funds were raised to buy more raw materials. By 1987, the work was reported to be in its last stages but the tall crane still dominated the scene, as it had done for ten years.

Within sight of the sea anglers, the kiln, a relic of the Brick and Tile Works, and which gave its name to Kiln Cottage, had been giving its owners cause for concern. There were serious doubts about the safety of its structure, covered as it was in ivy and with a hawthorn tree protruding

**The Brick and Tile Works' kiln restored.**
*Photo: John Upton. Village scrapbook.*

out of the top but it was the last of its kind in south-east England so it was decided to dismantle and rebuild it. The work was sponsored and administered by the Sussex Industrial Archaeological Group with eighty per cent of the work on site being done by members of the Lewes Archaeological Group, joined by two villagers. After a lifetime in insurance George Rowell turned himself into a most proficient steel bar bender and fixer and Eileen Howard's training as a biologist appeared to be no hindrance to her becoming a skilled brick pointer. Although all the labour was voluntary, the project cost £1,900 plus. The bulk of the money came from Lewes District Council, East Sussex County Council, the Civic Trust and the owners, the Wilkinson family. Thus Piddinghoe re-acquired a landmark, which remains as spruce today as it was in 1981, and possibly 1801 too.

Changes of a more subtle nature were taking place in the population of the parish. In 1981, roughly half were working (or seeking work), by 1991 the figure went up a few percentage points. The significant change, however, was among the rest, those not working. In 1981, just over a quarter were described as retired; by 1991 the proportion had risen to a half. If car ownership is anything to go by, Piddinghoers were also getting wealthier. Not only were there more two and three car households in the village in 1991 than 1981, but the 1991 figures were markedly more than the average for the district and county council areas. It is, of course, possible that a two-hourly bus service, daytime only, and never on a Sunday, might account for this situation. The figures also partly explain the amount of on-street parking in the village, especially at weekends; the other significant factor being the shortage of garages. Few of the old houses had space even for off-street parking, and car ownership cannot have been a consideration when Brookside was planned. More surprising is the apparent lack of foresight on the part of post-1960 developers and planners about the numbers of cars people were likely to have, especially those able to afford detached houses with four or five bedrooms.

The parish council continued to play its minor role in planning, passing its views up the administrative hierarchy to the district council. There were two proposed developments, in fields adjacent to the village, that aroused considerable feeling. Both were subsequently turned down. An earlier non-compliance with planning conditions ended, in July 1980, with one of the biggest fires ever seen in Piddinghoe, and one which brought the traffic on the main road to a standstill. Three years earlier a Newhaven man had bought an eight acre piece of land along the river north of Kiln Cottage for 'recreational and sporting purposes.' By the beginning of 1979 he had a caravan-workshop there and, with friends, was building a boat. He sought retrospective planning permission for the boat-building which was refused, even after an appeal. Not being able to afford to move the 51ft (15.7m) hull and its cradle, he poured petrol on it and set it alight, having previously alerted the *Evening Argus*. As huge clouds of black smoke billowed into the sky, he told a reporter:

> 'What you are witnessing is something like 3,500 hours of wasted effort and £4,000 in money. Just because somebody put the spoke in. I hope whoever is responsible for this ludicrous situation feels satisfied.'

In contrast to this dramatic outcome, the parish council's business was mainly routine and concerned with the same topics as in the previous two decades. Football continued on the Hoe, taking care of its mowing during the soccer season, and the children's play area was improved in 1986 by the addition of a log cabin slide and more swings.

The presence of the vicar, Geoffrey Holmes, in the village provided a visible, as well as spiritual, continuity to the decade. Sadly his wife, Elizabeth, died in December 1980. They married only six months before coming to Piddinghoe in 1976, when she was already suffering from a debilitating illness. She won admiration and affection from everyone for the courage she exhibited in continuing with her medical practice, as well as leading a full life in the parish. In her memory £730 was raised to go to one of her great interests, the hospice movement.

She loved children, and they responded warmly to her, to 'Dr Elizabeth' as they called her. The Sunday School she started with Jean Harper in November 1978 grew and flourished. She hoped it would be 'a sort-of Sunday club' which indeed it was. The children took part in village events, such as the Fayre, and singing carols round the houses at

Christmas, as well as contributing to the life of the church. With a show described as 'musical pot pourri' they raised £100 for the Elizabeth Holmes Memorial Window, which it had been decided to install in the church.

The Sunday School flourished for several years then numbers began to fall and it closed in 1986. Two and a half years later, with more children again in the village, John and Jean Harper re-opened their Sunday Club in the village hall. The vicar, meanwhile, was facing serious problems with his church's fabric. First the wooden shingles on the tower had to be replaced at an estimated cost of £900. Once again the Flower Festival came up trumps and raised £1,100, enabling the work to be completed within the month.

This was just the beginning. The bells could not be rung because at least one of them was in such a precarious position that it could fall; the flooring of the belfry was in poor condition;

**Alf Biggs and his young assistant Steven Bland, re-shingling the tower.** *Photo: Sussex Express*

and so were some of the beams of the tower and the west wall. However, in the course of examing the tower for defects, two of its beams were found to be dated 1271 and 1289.

A further £1,100 was needed for the repairs so once again fund-raising began in earnest. Event followed event, some organised by church

105

**The 1982 flower festival.**
*Photo: Village scrapbook.*

members, others by village groups, such as the Tennis Club's Bells' Auction which raised £205. Gradually, as the money came in, the work was completed, finally the bells were cleaned, and about to be rehung when cracks were found in the wall of the tower itself. However, before too long, even that was dealt with. Six months later the organ required restoration – likely cost £2,200, to include electrification of the pedal movement, while retaining the hand-blower for emergency use. Yet again, money-raising events proliferated, the final part of the debt being paid off by a dog show.

The flower festivals continued to be the church's major money spinner. They were now alternating with the produce and flower shows and from 1980 taking place on every second August Bank Holiday. With minor variations, tried and tested routines were followed. Flowers filled the church, stalls fringed the Green, paintings adorned the village hall, and in the afternoons, cream teas were served in village gardens. Profits rose to a spectacular £3,036 in 1988, but that was the year a car boot sale and musical evening had been added to the weekend's attractions.

Over the decade some £13,900 was also raised at events on the Hoe, of which £9,000 went to the church – not a bad total for a parish with about 200 people. The 1987 Village Fete and Dog Show provides an example of what else, other than money, such an event meant to a small community. From the village meeting on 5 February, which established that there was support for such an event and agreed the way forward, to the day itself – 27 June – the vast majority of the 200 people on the electoral roll had been involved, one way or another. The organising committee of eleven came from all parts of the village and everyone else was invited by letter to give their own ideas and offers of help. In addition to stallholders, it was estimated that sixty-eighty people would be required to assist with stalls and refreshments, six car parkers, eight to ten strong workhorses for setting up and clearing up, not forgetting the dog show and the barbecue. People worked co-operatively to tackle these tasks – some with friends, others with people they had scarcely seen before. Come the day there was the shared excitement, tinged with nervousness. Would it all work?

It did.

A similarly successful, but locals-only, jamboree had been held on 29 July 1981, the day of the Royal Wedding. During the afternoon, while thirty children were consuming a slap-up tea provided by Harry and Marion Cragg in the garden of the Royal Oak, followed by a treasure hunt organised by one of the mums, the tennis club's mixed doubles finals were being fought out on the Hoe. Novelty races followed, and an hour of rounders. Simultaneously six teams of six were locked in battle in a skittles tournament and in a close-run final the Court Farm Rollers (star bowler the vicar) beat the Brookside Under-21s. At dusk an enormous bonfire was lit at the far end of the Hoe, accompanied by a brilliant fire work display.

Between these big events, social life in the village continued much as before. The tennis club prospered with a membership between sixty and seventy and all the year round activity. The village hall kept its mix of regular and one-off activities. Interest evenings still attracted good audiences to their eclectic mix of topics, even though the price of admission rose from 30p in 1980 to 75p in 1989. Ten years of fortnightly whist came to an end in 1983, as did the small branch library three years later. It had been established soon after the hall opened and the County Library Service changed the 300 books every three months. By 1986 this had lengthened to every six months so the village asked for the Mobile Library to call instead. The demise of the library coincided with difficulties in the WI. Up to 1985 it had a full programme of events and activities but then membership fell away, until in November 1987 it closed down.

Only a month before, Piddinghoe, along with hundreds of other places in the south, thought that far more than the WI was coming to an end. Thursday 16 October 1987 was the night of the hurricane. After several hours of screaming wind, and just a few subsequent hours of fitful sleep, it was with considerable trepidation that curtains were drawn the next morning, For many, the scene before them was completely different from the one they had left the night before. Compared to many places Piddinghoe was fortunate, although damage was still being repaired months later. The immediate problem was loss of electric power – in a parish with no mains gas. Solid fuel cookers and candles reigned supreme, just as they had for the first forty years of the century. After eight or eleven days, depending on location, everyone was much relieved when power again flowed at the flick of a switch.

# 11

# END OF AN ERA – AND THE ROYAL OAK

## 1990–99

The Nineties were politically volatile; from the dramatic departure of Margaret Thatcher in November 1990, to the sudden death of Labour leader John Smith in 1994, setting Tony Blair on the road to New Labour's landslide victory in the 1997 General Election. Only four months later the nation was stunned by the news of the tragic death of the Princess of Wales which produced an unparalleled outburst of national mourning.

The communication revolution of the Eighties swept on into the Nineties. This was the decade of the Internet, the World Wide Web, E-mail and a proliferation of dot-com addresses, as well as the National Lottery which drew a huge television audience on its opening night of 20 November 1994. As technological advancement in communications had its pluses and minuses, so too the many developments in science: Dolly, the cloned sheep, raised hopes of medical breakthroughs but fears of genetic manipulation.

The Nineties enabled many people, if they so chose, to spend seven days a week on their favourite hobby. From December 1993 shops could open on a Sunday if their owners so wished and by the end of the decade, some were open throughout the day and night. Not that this was of much interest to the people of Piddinghoe, being now without a shop of any sort. And worse was to come. The event which finally made the

**The pub a few years after the fire, with its windows boarded up, a tarpaulin on its roof and a collapsed string of coloured lights hanging across the 'family garden'.**
*Photo: Village scrapbook*

village purely residential was a fire at the Royal Oak. In the early evening of a cold, dark Sunday in January 1992 flames were seen through the back windows, licking up the walls and the curtains. The first most people knew about it was when the fire engines arrived, blocking The Street, their vivid blue lights flashing across the scene. There was no one on the premises and firefighters set about dousing the flames and hacking holes through the roof, through which billowed acrid smoke.

Thus began a saga which would last almost four years. There were newspaper stories about the 'mystery' fire at the Royal Oak. Arson was a suggested cause and there followed a lengthy dispute between creditors and insurers. At first, the building from the front looked undamaged. At lunchtime, prospective customers would wait patiently outside, glancing at their watches once or twice, until they looked inside, and were amazed at what they saw. Each table in the restaurant was laid ready for a meal, with knives, forks, wine glasses and napkins – all coated in a layer of black soot, as were the walls and ceiling.

The roof was becoming a hazard as in windy weather slates would come crashing down. It was sheeted over with a blue tarpaulin which flapped and eventually tore, letting the slates again escape. Eventually the windows were boarded up and by 1994 rats had taken up residence. 'What is happening to the Oak?' became the most frequently-heard question in the village. 'Is it for sale? If not, why not?' For three years the most prominent building on The Street gradually deteriorated. Then, early in 1995, came a dual planning application for change of use from licensed to residential premises, and for the building of a large second house in the garden. The Oak had been bought by a developer.

There was immediate opposition 'in principle and in detail' from the parish council. Letters were written, a 100-name petition presented and the application was refused. Within days the developer said he was willing to sell the Oak to anyone able to keep it open. Both sides knew that finding such a person or organisation would be difficult because of the competition pubs were facing from the all-day availability of beers, wines and spirits from supermarkets and, since the introduction of the breathalyser, people's increasing preference for having a drink at home. A scheme was launched to try to buy the Oak as a community pub/centre. Parish support was overwhelming. Many offered practical help, some, financial assistance, but £150,000 was needed. The search area for support was widened via local radio and TV but to no avail. The money could not be found.

In December 1995 new conversion plans were submitted, which, after revision, were approved. A later application, for a smaller second house, was refused. Onto the market in August 1996 came a 'highly desirable' five bed-roomed house and just before Christmas lights were blazing from its windows. A family with two children had moved in, blissfully unaware of the history of the previous four years.

In addition to the Royal Oak conversion, three new houses were built in the village, and the first three of eight in former barns at Hoddern Farm, high on Lodge Hill. Chapel Barn at Deans was also converted

111

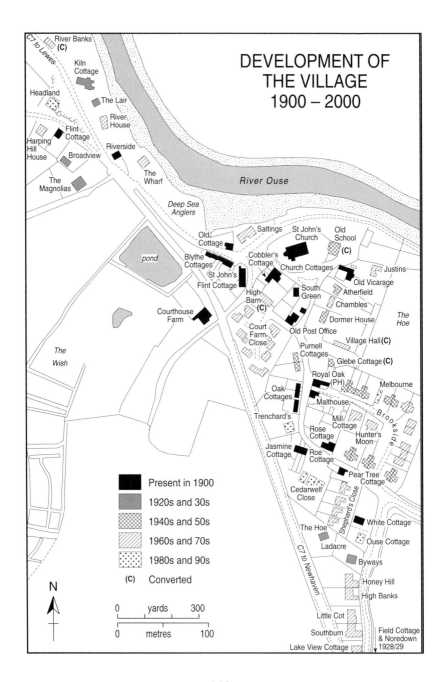

# DEVELOPMENT OF THE VILLAGE 1900 – 2000

C7 to Lewes

River Banks **(C)**
Kiln Cottage
Headland
The Lair
River House
Flint Cottage
Harping Hill House
Broadview
Riverside
The Magnolias
The Wharf

River Ouse

Deep Sea Anglers

pond

Old Cottage
Saltings
St John's Church
Old School **(C)**
Blythe Cottages
Cobbler's Cottage
Church Cottages
Justins
St John's Flint Cottage
High Barn **(C)**
South Green
Old Vicarage
Atherfield
Chambles
Courthouse Farm
Dormer House
The Hoe
Court Farm Close
Old Post Office
Village Hall **(C)**
Purnell Cottages
Glebe Cottage **(C)**
The Wish
Royal Oak (PH)
Melbourne
Oak Cottages
Malthouse
Brookside
Trenchard's
Mill Cottage
Rose Cottage
Hunter's Moon
Jasmine Cottage
Roe Cottage
Pear Tree Cottage
Cedarwell Close
Shepherd's Close
White Cottage
The Hoe
Ouse Cottage
C7 to Newhaven
Ladacre
Byways
Honey Hill
High Banks
Little Cot
Southburn
Lake View Cottage
Field Cottage & Noredown 1928/29

| | |
|---|---|
| ■ (black) | Present in 1900 |
| ■ (grey) | 1920s and 30s |
| ▨ (crosshatch) | 1940s and 50s |
| ▨ (diagonal) | 1960s and 70s |
| ⠿ (dotted) | 1980s and 90s |
| **(C)** | Converted |

N

0 — yards — 300
0 — metres — 100

112

into a fine home. Between them they brought in twelve additional people, although for one it was a return to the place of his birth and childhood. Arrivals were more than balanced, however, by departures. In 1998 there had been 207 names on the electoral roll, by 1999 this number had dropped to 201. Adding to these names those of resident children and young people gives a total parish population of 231 – exactly the same number as in the census for 1901.

The circumstances in which these 231 lived were, however, very different. In 1999 these Piddinghoers occupied 107 homes, more than ninety per cent of them owner-occupied. In 1901 the same number crowded into about fifty dwellings, the vast majority of them rented. More than seventy per cent of these end-of-century Piddinghoers came to the parish in the last twenty years, some seventeen per cent in the Sixties and Seventies, the remainder prior to 1960. Descendants of the old families are still to be found. In 1999 eight Penfolds, one of whom is also a Stace, three Bennetts, and two Carrs; the elders being ninety six-year old  Olive Crooks (a Penfold) and, in their eighties, Mary Woolger neé Bennett and Frank Stace, the son of the wheelchair-bound soccer fan of the Sixties, Mrs Olive Stace.

During the decade Piddinghoe lost two of its outstanding characters. For more than forty years Daisy Paddy had given enthusiastic and practical support to every kind of church activity. At the Fayres the tea tent was Daisy's province – she would always be commandingly positioned behind a large teapot. She died on 19 February 1991 and by a village subscription a wrought-iron flower stand was purchased and placed in her memory in the church which she loved. Just seven years later, on 23 February 1998, Molly Pelling died, aged sixty-six. She was of the next generation to Daisy Paddy but as well known in her different way. She was a

**Daisy Paddy**

113

true Piddinghoer, the third generation on both sides of her family to live and work in the parish. For the last twenty-one years of her life she was

the village 'papergirl' on duty seven days a week in all weathers. In many ways she epitomised the 'old' village. It had always been her whole world in which she did countless untold kindnesses. The response of villagers to her final, grievous illness, epitomised the best of the 'new' village, a community which cared deeply and which gave every kind of practical help. Outside her old home a seat, paid for by public subscription, commemorates her life.

**Molly Pelling outside Court House Farm in 1958**

The availability for conversion of so much barn space at Hoddern was an indication of the changing face of agriculture, not just in Piddinghoe. From the Twenties onwards, the crops grown and animals reared had been much affected by government, and later, European policies. Increased production in the Seventies resulted in the infamous 'food mountains' of the Eighties. Consequent reductions in quotas and other support mechanisms signalled a downwards slide in farm fortunes not seen since the depression of the early Thirties. Diversification became the watchword. Farmers had to find other sources of income, other uses for land.

Wherever there was a vibrant housing market, as in Sussex, there was a demand for redundant farm buildings. Hoddern also had its extensive stabling for the keeping of horses – an alternative enterprise much favoured in areas adjacent to an urban population. Additionally, the Carr brothers turned to rearing game birds and organising shoots. In common with many other local farmers, they also put some of their fields down to rape and later linseed, bringing vivid patches of yellow and misty blue to the countryside. They increased their number of ewes and sheep and their lambs bleating in the fields around the village was a nostalgic reminder of the old days. Soon two further problems were to hit the nation's farmers. The BSE crisis devastated the cattle and beef trade and later adverse financial exchange rates, affected many aspects of agriculture. There was also increasing public concern for the environment; of which, in the countryside, farmers were the chief custodians.

In 1991 the Countryside Commission selected the Sussex Downs Area of Outstanding Natural Beauty for a new, experimental, management framework. The following year the Sussex Downs Conservation Board came into being for a trial period of six years, by agreement between the Commission and the thirteen local authorities involved. Piddinghoe benefited in various ways from contacts with the new Board, acquiring, for example, new 'kissing' gates along the river path in place of derelict stiles. In 1998 the Board's remit was extended to allow more time for a decision on its continuance or replacement. In 1999 the Secretary of State for the Environment recommended that the Sussex Downs become a National Park, although challenges to this decision continue.

A major feature of the village environment had long been the Hoe, bought originally by the parish council as a sports field. For seventy years football had been played there by a succession of local and neighbouring clubs – until 1995 when, in a friendly match before the start of the season, a player broke his ankle, allegedly catching his foot in a hole. As a consequence, the Sunday League would not use the pitch again unless it was improved. After taking professional advice, the parish council decided that it was not a viable proposition to improve the ground and that was the end of football on the Hoe. There was also concern for the safety of the children's play area. An inspection by a Lewes District Council officer in 1994 confirmed that it no longer met current standards and it was agreed that a completely new play area should be built. A year later, after endless consultations, meetings, form filling-in, and a grant of £10,000 from Lewes District Council, the new play area was in use. It has continued to be immensely popular with both Piddinghoe children and visitors.

The management of the Hoe was causing some financial difficulty.

**The swings, slide and climbing frame of the new play area are given a definite seal of approval by the youngsters clambering over them.** *Photo: Village scrapbook.*

Loss of the regular renting-out contract not only cut off a source of revenue but caused additional expenditure because the grass now had to be cut in spring and autumn as well as summer. The parish council, which had prided itself on not having to seek a precept, in 1992 had to ask the district council to collect for it the sum of £500. Each year thereafter a precept was charged, in 1996 to include paying for the provision of bus passes. At a cost of £8 to the recipient, these were taken up by some ten or eleven over sixties each year. Coincidentally, in October 1999, the number of weekday buses to Newhaven and Lewes nearly doubled, so giving the village its best service for many years.

At the same time that questions were being asked about the future of the Royal Oak, concern was simmering over developments at the church. In 1993, Geoffrey Holmes decided to move, prior to his retirement, to a group of more rural parishes in West Sussex. At this time Peacehaven was also without a vicar and rumours were rife that the parishes were to be re-organised and one church would close. Would it be the one at Piddinghoe?

Originally the diocese had favoured linking the six parishes of the Ouse Valley, from Kingston to Piddinghoe, a scheme to which Kingston was implacably opposed. The alternative was joining the united benefice of Telscombe, Piddinghoe and Southease to Peacehaven and this it did. On 4 September 1994 the Reverend David Hider, newly-appointed vicar of Peacehaven, was licensed as priest-in-charge of the three rural parishes, including Piddinghoe. He was to have two ordained assistants to help him, one of whom would be assigned to the rural parishes. The churchwardens from these parishes urged the Bishop and Archdeacon to buy a property in one of the villages to serve the rural area, and, late in 1995, a house was bought in Piddinghoe. However, no appointment was made and a rota of priests continued to serve St John's. Then in September 1996, the Reverend David Perks, assistant to the Rural Dean, agreed to take the post as part-time assistant curate. As he lived in Lewes, the house in the village was let.

The proposed parish re-organisation seemed almost an irrelevance to those trying to cope with the age-old problem of keeping St John's in a reasonable state of repair. In 1990 examination revealed another £6,000 worth of infestation with 'wood-boring insects', nearly twice as much as was in the coffers. In 1991, inspection moved on to the roof of the nave. There some timbers needed to be replaced and the Diocesan Advisory Committee recommended the use of stainless steel, for which the total bill would be £26,620. For a church with a small congregation and a parish of some 200 people these were mind-blowing sums. Yet they were found.

The major fund-raiser continued to be the bi-ennial flower festivals, run throughout the Nineties, as they had been since the Seventies, by Sheila Redman and her husband, Martin. There had long been a preceding event, a ploughman's lunch and auction, but with the vast sums now required, the August Bank Holiday itself, in 1992 and 1994, had 'fringe activities'. On the Saturday mornings there was a car boot sale on the Hoe and on the Sunday evenings a concert of music in St John's. By these means, these two festivals together raised £7,857.18 –

**Youngest and oldest in the village hall. Baby Samantha, asleep in the arms of her
mother Hilary Buck, and eighty-nine year old Mrs Olive Crooks.
Below: The Good Friday tradition of long rope skipping was revived in the 1990s.**
*Photos: Village scrapbook.*

the total over the decade being £17,079.40.

In addition to these big events, there were dozens of smaller ones, organised by groups and individuals 'for the church roof'. Bearing in mind that not everyone wanted, nor was able, to contribute to this relentless activity, it tended to be the same people who devoted a disproportionate amount of time and energy to a church, which some of them rarely, if ever, attended. Even before the roof was paid for, other work was identified. Fund-raising continued, including inserting single-day fetes in both 1995 and 1997. Although the first of these raised more than £1,000, a discernible fete-fatigue was becoming evident.

The suggestion therefore that a charitable organisation, the Friends of St John's, might be formed, was timely. A village meeting of some fifty people, in March 1998, enthusiastically supported its formation with the object of 'restoring, preserving and improving' St John's church and 'raising funds towards the payments of accounts for work done . . .'

That other Piddinghoe institution, the village hall, had a successful decade, financially as well as socially. Safety work was carried out, as well as refurbishment of the main room, to a standard much admired by visitors as well as villagers. All the regular activities of the Eighties continued through the Nineties. The Mothers and Toddlers Group had a slight hiccup in 1992 when it ran out of children. A year later, however, there were again two or three, so activities resumed, since when it has not looked back. By May 1996 there were nine mothers (six from in and around Piddinghoe) with ten toddlers aged from ten months to three years. By the end of the decade, in addition to three recently-born, four other village babies were expected, ready to replace the older ones as they go on to nursery school.

There was also the usual mix of one-off events. One of these was re-introduction of the traditional Good Friday Long Rope Skipping, albeit now lasting only an hour or so instead of most of the day, and followed by coffee and hot-cross buns in the village hall. In later years, other Easter activities for children were added, but the skipping itself now attracts quite a few visitors. The major innovation, however, was the Royal Oak Survivors' Club. With the demise of the pub a group of its old regulars had come up with the idea –and the name. They wanted to turn the village hall, periodically, into a pub. Initially some reactions were wary. After all it could be a financial disaster, if nothing worse. However it was decided to give it a go, and the rest, as they say is history. On fifteen days, mostly Saturdays associated with a seasonal event, between 20 September 1997 and New Year's Eve 1999, more people packed into the transformed and 'occasionally licensed' village hall, than had been in the real Oak for some time prior to the fire.

Less successful was the WI. In 1990 a few former members thought it worth trying to start again, others agreed and a full programme of meetings, events and outings was arranged, albeit for only ten members. A year later no one else could be persuaded to join, indeed one had left, so by December 1992 they had, again, to call it a day.

Tennis proved altogether more popular. Membership of the club peaked in mid-decade at over seventy, forty being playing members: although this dropped to thirty-nine by 1999, thirty of them were regular players, plus six juniors.The court continued to be in use all year round, and the year's programme still included social events and visits to the David Lloyd Centre at Eastbourne. An innovation was an annual stoolball match, Tennis Club versus Village, which always lives up to the club's claim that its object is enjoyment rather than competition.

The sailing club continued to flourish. Members were particularly proud of their cadet section, for which the sheltered waters of the Pond were especially suitable. Over the years hundreds of youngsters learned to sail there, including Neal MacDonald who lived in the village as a boy, and who, in 1997, was one of the crew of *Silk Cut,* the British entry in the Whitbread Challenge Round-the-World race. On Monday evenings villagers learned to approach the southern end of the village with care, as scores of cars sped in to turn down the bumpy track to the Pond. The youngsters looked forward to Cadet Week in the summer, during which there were races and waterbourne games. In 1990 there were celebrations at the scene of Piddinghoe's other waterbourne activity – the Deep Sea Anglers wharf was officially opened. Three years later a toilet block and locker room was added to their site.

*The Villager*, a bi-monthly magazine written by and for Piddinghoers, first appeared in May 1996. It carried no advertisements and was largely about the parish. Its instigator and producer, Ken Cheeseman, originally visited every home in the parish. Four years on, its subscription list still included almost every household and 100 individuals had contributed articles. This suggests a high level of interest in and commitment to the parish, a characteristic also born out by the success of the Royal Oak Survivors and various village events, including those which took Piddinghoers from 1999 into 2000.

Almost every person in the village physically able to be there was present at some time between the evening of 31 December 1999 and the afternoon of 1 January 2000. For some the festivities began and ended in the village hall, in its guise as the Royal Oak. However, approaching the midnight hour on New Year's Eve they joined one of the noisy mobs which set off from each end of the dark village, candles and lanterns held high. Meeting at the entrance to the Hoe, the mood changed.

In pitch blackness, bobbing lights advanced silently over the grass, wave upon wave of muffled figures looming up towards the glow of the bonfire. Momentarily it could have been the tenth century not the twentieth. Big Ben, church bells, fireworks and plenty of hugs ushered in the new century. After savouring the moment out there on the dark Hoe, gradually people returned to their homes, especially those with children, while others returned to the warmth and congeniality of the village hall. Next day, at 12.15pm, a full congregation in St John's shared in a short service, the ancient building itself symbolising for all a reassuring continuity of spirit and purpose. Then it was all out onto Church Bank where more than 100 people had gathered for the unveiling of Piddinghoe's Millennium Monument – a 12ft high pole on which is mounted a segmented globe bearing the name 'Piddinghoe' in gilded letters. On top of the globe floats a fat gold fish weathervane. It was designed by Ken Cheeseman, made by Lewes blacksmith Ben Autie and paid for by parish subscription.

Taped patriotic music filled the air, gasps of pleasure and clapping greeted the golden fish and the globe as they emerged when the cover was removed, with a certain amount of difficulty, by two young villagers, Claire Barker and Samantha Buck. Short speeches were made and a time capsule placed in the base by Mary Woolger, more than eighty years a Piddinghoer. The crowd clasped hands to sing *Auld Lang Syne* before crowding round to read the inscription on the metal strip which is wound round the pole:

ERECTED
SATURDAY
THE
FIRST
DAY
OF
JANUARY
IN
THE
YEAR
TWO
THOUSAND
A.D.
TO
CELEBRATE
THE
ARRIVAL
OF
A
NEW
MILLENNIUM.

# Appendix 1

## ST JOHN'S CHURCH – VICARS 1900–2000

| *From* | *To* | |
|--------|------|--|
| 1894 | | William George Trousdale |
| 1901 | 1910 | Frederic John Poole |
| 1910 | | William Arnold Carr |
| 1912 | 1926 | George Street |
| 1926 | 1931 | George Preston Kelsall Winlaw |
| 1931 | 1962 | Henry Martyn Harries |
| 1963 | 1976 | Richard Derek Payne |
| 1976 | 1993 | Robert John Geoffrey Holmes |
| 1994 | | David A Hider, Vicar of Peacehaven, Priest-in-Charge of Piddinghoe. |

## PIDDINGHOE PAROCHIAL SCHOOL

Head Teachers

| | |
|--|--|
| 1881-1908 | Miss Lucy Atwood, became Mrs Baker in 1887 |
| 1908-1911 | Miss Ella Pearman |
| 1911-1912 | Miss Bere |
| 1912-1914 | Miss E E Warren |
| 1915-1915 | Miss May Young |
| 1915-1923 | Miss Daisy Iris Porter |
| 1923-1925 | Mrs Agnes Furness |
| 1925-1946 | Mrs Jane Muir |
| 1947-1951 | Miss Josephine Jenner |
| 1951-1952 | Mrs R M Vinall |

Assistant teachers

| | |
|--|--|
| 1893- 1927 | Miss Martha Parker |
| 1909-1919 | Miss Lilian King |
| 1919-1921 | Miss Maud Bennett |
| 1927-1930 | Miss Muriel Winter |
| 1932-1941 | Mrs Rita Cook, became Mrs Chapman in 1938 |
| 1941-1947 | Mrs Sampford, became Mrs Nelson Hills in 1946 |

# APPENDIX 11

## Extracts from Farm Survey 4 June 1941

|  |  | Deans | Court House | Hoddern |
|---|---|---|---|---|
| % farm naturally | good | 75 | 40 | 25 |
|  | fair | 25 | 50 | 50 |
|  | bad |  | 10 | 25 |
| Condition of arable | % good | 75 | 50 |  |
|  | % fair | 25 | 50 | 100 |
| Condition of pasture | % good | 60 | 50 |  |
|  | % fair | 27.5 | 50 | 100 |
|  | % poor | 12.5 |  |  |
| No. of cattle |  | 94 | 59 | 49 |
| No of poultry |  | 100 | 55 | 380 |
| No of pigs |  | 4 |  |  |
| No. of horses | for work | 11 | 4 | 3 |
|  | other | 3 |  |  |
| Tractors |  | 2 | 2 | 1 |
| Electricity |  | yes | no | no |
| Condition of buildings (excluding house) |  | good | mostly bad | fair |
| Management of resources |  | A | B | B |

# PARISH FACTS AND FIGURES

## Acreage

| 1900-1929 | Post 1934 |
|---|---|
| 2,347acres | 1,047acres |

## Local government

| 1900-1934 | 1934 | 1974 |
|---|---|---|
| Newhaven RDC | Newhaven RDC taken into Chailey RDC | Chailey RDC taken into new Lewes District |

## Population

| 1901 | 1911 | 1921 | 1931 | 1941 | 1951 | 1961 | 1971 | 1981 | 1991 | 1999(est) |
|---|---|---|---|---|---|---|---|---|---|---|
| 231 | 250 | 202 | 204 | no data | 214 | 197 | 233 | 245 | 230 | 231 |

# SOURCES

## Books, journals, theses and maps

Abbey Guide. *Sussex Downland and Sea Coast.* Abbey Publicity Service *c*1937
Bell, C R V *A History of East Sussex County Council.* Phillimore 1975
Brandon, P and Short, B. *The South East from AD 1000.* Longman 1990
Burgess, P and Saunders , A. *Battle Over Sussex.* Middleton Press 1990
Copper, R. *A Song for Every Season.* Paladin 1971
Copper, R. *Bob Copper's Sussex.* S.B.Publications 1997
Corbishley, G. *Ration Book Recipes.* English Heritage 1991
Crook, P. *Sussex Home Guard.* Middleton Press 1998
D'Enno, D. *The Saltdean Story.* Phillimore 1985
Farrant, J. 'The Lower Ouse Navigation pt II' in *Sussex Industrial Archaeology Newsletter No 4* October 1974
Farrant, S P. *The role of landowners and tenants in changing agricultural practice in the valley of the River Ouse, south of Lewes (Sussex) 1780-1930 and the consequences for the landscape.* Unpublished PhD thesis, London University 1977
Garcia, P 'A Feminine View of the Reconstruction Work at Piddinghoe'. *Lewes Archaeological Group Newsletter No.56.* May 1981
Hill, A. *Lower Ouse Navigation 1934-1967.* Hill 1991
Lucas, E V. *Highways and Byways in Sussex.* Macmillan 1904 and 1935
Metcalfe, R E.*The Lower Ouse Basin, Sussex.* University of London, unpublished dissertation 1953
Newby, H. *Country Life: A Social History of Rural England* Weidenfeld and Nicholson 1987
O'Shea, E W. 'The Restoration of a Tile Kiln at Piddinghoe' *Sussex Industrial History No.12* 1982
Poplett, R. *Peacehaven: A Pictorial History.* Phillimore 1993
Sussex Express and County Herald's *The War in East Sussex.* 1945
Ordnance Survey Maps, 1899 onwards

## Documents

Public Record Office, Kew.
1  Inland Revenue Valuation (Lloyd George's *Domesday).* Piddinghoe field book and map, mostly completed 2 July 1914.
2  National Farm Survey of England and Wales 1940-43. Piddinghoe field books and maps.

East Sussex Record Office. Lewes

1 Farm sale details: Friar's Bay Farm 25 October 1910; part of Chichester Estate, Lot 8 Deans Farm, Lot 9 Hoddern Farm 1912/3; Hoddern Farm 17 October 1977.

2 Register of farms and other premises used as dairies. Chailey Rural District Council 1926-35.

3 Diary of a landgirl at Dean's Farm, November 1939-January 1940.

4 Piddinghoe School admission register 1909-1952; log book 1913-1952; managers' minutes 1901-1942.

5 Minutes of church meetings and accounts 1924-26.

6 Census returns 1901-1991

7 Annual electoral rolls 1900-1999; no data 1916-1918 and 1940-1944

Newhaven Historical Society

Agreement between Newhaven and Seaford Water company and Newhaven Rural District Council for extension of water main to Piddinghoe, 20 September 1911.

Further extension to Harpin Hill 21 June 1912.

Piddinghoe

St John's Church Registers, Baptism, Marriage and Burial 1900-1999.

Parish magazine. Extracts 1904-1910; 1946 April-October; 1950 July. All issues from October 1961-December 1999 (from 1977 the magazine was called *Downland Review).*

Parish council minutes and papers 1955-1999.

Village hall minutes and papers 1973-1999.

Village and WI scrapbooks.

Farm sale catalogues.

Newspapers

*East Sussex News, Sussex County Herald, Southern Weekly News, Sussex Express, Evening Argus.*

# INDEX